Praise for *Confessions of a S*

"*Confessions of a Scholarship Winner* is a ...
who wants to learn more about the financial-aid and scholarship
process for attending a college or university. Kristina's personal story is
both compelling and accessible, and her clear, thoughtful writing helps
makes this an indispensable resource for the college-bound student."

Dr. Thomas Burns
Provost, Belmont University

"Kristina Ellis's story is absolutely inspiring. And the 'insider' information
she presents in this book is just as motivating. If you're looking for great
ideas and easy-to-follow advice from somebody who has already blazed
the scholarship trail, Kristina Ellis is *the* choice. *Confessions of a Scholarship
Winner* is the only book you'll need for creating your own path to success."

Curt Jones
Founder & CEO, Dippin' Dots Ice Cream

"I love this easy-to-follow guide for finding and winning scholarships.
Confessions of a Scholarship Winner is packed with information, yet
it is presented so well that it's not intimidating. It's a fast read and
easy to implement. Homeschool.com highly recommends it."

Rebecca Kochenderfer
Senior Editor and Co-Founder,
Homeschool.com, Inc.

"I wish I had been given a copy of this book in high school—
what an incredible resource for young people! Now everyone
will understand that going to college really doesn't have to
leave you or your family in debt for years. Students and parents
alike need to read *Confessions of a Scholarship Winner*!"

Brenna Mader
Miss Tennessee USA 2013

Confessions of a SCHOLARSHIP WINNER

The Secrets That
Helped Me Win
$500,000 in Free
Money for College

How You Can Too!

KRISTINA ELLIS

WORTHY
PUBLISHING

Published by Worthy Books, an imprint of Worthy Publishing Group, a division of Worthy Media, Inc., One Franklin Park, 6100 Tower Circle, Suite 210, Franklin, TN 37067.

HELPING PEOPLE EXPERIENCE THE HEART OF GOD

eBook available at worthypublishing.com

Audio distributed through Brilliance Audio; visit brillianceaudio.com

Library of Congress Control Number: 2012956458

For foreign and subsidiary rights, contact Riggins International Rights Service, Inc., rigginsrights.com

Published in association with David Sams Corporation

ISBN: 978-1-61795-157-2 (trade paper)

Cover Design: Christopher Tobias, Tobias Outerwear for Books
Interior Typesetting: Susan Browne Design

Printed in USA

16 17 18 19 LBM 16 15 14 13 12

I dedicate this book to
the students God had in mind
when he inspired me to write it . . .

To those who long for an education
but don't know how to pay for it.

And to those with big dreams
who are searching for a way to reach them.

May this book provide you with
the tools and inspiration you need
to reach your goals.

CONTENTS

A NOTE TO STUDENTS

If you're reading this book, you can win scholarships. Yes, *you*! Don't worry if you don't have perfect grades or aren't a star athlete. And don't think your family's financial status—whether it's poverty level, middle class, or wealthy—can keep you from getting free money for college. Scholarships are available for nearly everything! Millions of dollars are given away every year to students from all backgrounds and for all sorts of reasons! Somebody is going to get them. It might as well be you!

As you've gotten closer to graduating from high school, you've probably started dreaming about going to a great university and having the infamous college experience. Unfortunately, those dreams can seem short-lived when you come face-to-face with the reality that COLLEGE IS EXPENSIVE! If you're looking at your family's financial situation along with rising tuition costs and thinking, *There's no way I could ever afford this!* . . . well, think again.

Many of your peers will end up settling for a minimal college experience, massive amounts of student loans, or no education at all. I was headed down the same path until one life-changing challenge from my mother on my first day of high school. She believed I could go to the university of my dreams *and* get scholarships to pay for it. She saw a future for me that was well beyond the huge obstacles confronting our family at that time. By casting a wider vision for my life, she set me on a journey I couldn't have imagined would be possible.

It is a vision I want to hold out to you as not just *possible* but *well within your reach*. I'm also offering in this book what neither my mother nor I had at the time: a map to discovering hidden treasure—free money for college.

Think of the scholarship process like a game. One offering huge prizes to the winners—literally, hundreds of thousands of dollars each year. In this book, I explain the secrets and strategies that turn ordinary kids like me into scholarship winners.

Contrary to what you may have heard, you don't have to be a valedictorian, class president, or star athlete to be a great scholarship candidate. I'm living proof that scholarships aren't just for the supersmart or ultratalented, and that your current situation doesn't have to determine your final destination! With hard work, dedication, and the insider information in these pages, I was able to win over half a million dollars in scholarships and attend the university of my choice *for free*! I'm confident that you too can find tremendous scholarship success and begin the journey toward the future of your dreams. It is all about effectively presenting what makes you unique and desirable as a scholarship candidate—and I'm here to show you how to do that.

In these pages, I go one step further, not only giving you the how-to tips of the scholarship process but also sharing my story so you can know who I am, where I've been, how alike we probably are, and why I care so much about your future. That's why it's called *"Confessions" of a Scholarship Winner*. This book is full of confessions from my life and my scholarship journey, as well as from the journeys of other students who earned scholarships for college.

I've devoted *Confessions of a Scholarship Winner* to every one of you who needs help finding money for college and who is dedicated to transforming your future. Maybe you feel ordinary or can't see past the circumstances you're in now, but you have extraordinary potential.

I pray that this book will give you the encouragement and the resources you need to go after all your dreams. Together, we can create a strategy that will help you stand out to scholarship committees in the best way possible and achieve the success you deserve!

I'm with you in this!

Your scholarship mentor,

Kristina Ellis

A NOTE TO PARENTS

I know from experience how important you can be to your teen's success. While sometimes students try to "play it cool" and act like you don't matter, you really do. This is especially true in the scholarship application process.

As you'll read in my story (chapter 1), my mom's encouragement is what influenced me to start working for scholarships in the first place. I will forever be so grateful to her for inspiring me to believe in myself, for being honest and open about what I'd be up against in college, and for doing everything she could to guide me through.

She helped me find the best scholarships to apply for, kept me organized, and was a great sounding board. She would come hang out with me at the library, making sure I was taking fun breaks throughout the night. She made what could have been a boring process for a high school student feel like we were having our own party!

My mom and I already had a great relationship prior to my preparation for college, but the scholarship quest brought us even closer. What my mom couldn't give me financially out of her own pocket, she made up for with love and motivation. And with her standing by me, I was able to overcome every obstacle I faced and win over half a million dollars in scholarships, providing funding through a doctoral degree. I also was able to attend Vanderbilt University for free—one of the top private schools in the country!

Parents, you know your student better than anyone else, and you want to cheer him or her on more than anyone else. I encourage you to begin by sitting down with your son or daughter and doing what my mom did with me: have a real conversation about the future and how you can make college dreams a reality. You can start with the principles and secrets I share in this book. Then simply let your teenager know that you believe in his or her potential for success and you are there to offer support throughout the scholarship process.

There may be times when your teenager feels overwhelmed, unmotivated, or just generally frustrated. Don't let him or her give up! The extra encouragement and love they get from you can make all the difference on the road to winning scholarships. Together, you can make it happen!

Sincerely,

Kristina Ellis

P.S. Please refer to "How Parents Can Help" in the Resources section at the back of the book for specific ways you can effectively team up with your student for success.

I CONFESS . . .

The Imperfect Life of a Scholar

The pounding on the front door echoed throughout our house, and I instantly knew I was in trouble. The towering figure in the window looked very angry. Tears began streaming down my face as I hid in the coat closet, fearful of my impending punishment. As a third grader, breaking my neighbor's swing set felt like an epic disaster. I was terrified, knowing she had come to my house to make sure I paid dearly for it. I pressed my ear to the door as hard as I could but still couldn't hear anything. Mustering up every ounce of courage I had, I slipped out of the closet and tiptoed over to peek through the open front door.

I was surprised and confused to see tears streaming down my mother's face. I had never seen my mom cry—not even after my dad's death just a few months earlier.

I'll never forget the haunting words my neighbor sarcastically said to my mom: "Go back where you came from! There's no way you can survive in the United States without your husband! Just take your kids back to Venezuela with you. At least there, they'd have a chance of living a normal life."

Thankfully, "normal" wasn't good enough for my mom. She took those searing words from an angry neighbor and turned them into . . . *motivation.* Instead of being paralyzed by obstacles or defeated by circumstances, my mother accepted them as challenges. And in her mind, challenges are meant to be overcome.

Finding the Way Through

My life has had plenty of struggles, doubts, and moments of feeling I wasn't good enough to reach my dreams. Yet somehow I stand here today, realizing I *am* good enough and my dreams *have* come true.

On the surface, some people might call my story "luck" because, despite the odds against me, I beat them. People have wondered if maybe I was always in the right place at the right time. Oftentimes I was, but how did I get there? Did I stumble my way into success? Did I aimlessly wander until I had "arrived"? Absolutely not!

I learned from my mom that with hard work and the right strategy, you can achieve success no matter what obstacles are standing in your way. When difficulties arise, there *is* always a way through. Sometimes, you just have to keep trying different paths until the next step becomes clear.

My mom's determination and positive outlook helped shape

my attitude and influenced how I handled difficult situations. She laid the foundation for me to be able to overcome the obstacles I faced growing up. Now I get to pass on to you not only the secrets to scholarship success that I discovered on my road to college but also some encouragement for whatever difficulties you might be up against. I can do this because by the time I graduated from high school, I'd battled and overcome some of the most significant challenges any young person can endure.

The very beginning of my story, though, was nearly perfect.

I was born into a wonderful, happy family. My dad was a small-town man from Vincennes, Indiana, who loved music and built guitars. My mother moved to the United States from Venezuela to go to college. My parents met at our local college—Vincennes University—and quickly fell in love and got married. A few years later, they had my brother, and then two and a half years later, I came along.

Though our family didn't have a ton of money, we were comfortable and happy.

Then, just as my parents were hoping to add a third child to our family, our storybook beginning took a terrible turn. My mom was awakened in the middle of the night by my dad convulsing in the bed next to her. In a state of sheer panic, she frantically dialed 911. Moments later, the paramedics swarmed into our home and rushed him to the hospital.

My dad had no prior health issues, so both my parents were

completely blindsided when the doctors diagnosed him with a cancerous brain tumor. That night began a journey that no family ever plans on taking.

I was three at the time, but I still remember so many painful details. Dad's symptoms revealed themselves very slowly at first, but soon seizures and chemotherapy became part of our everyday routine. By age five, I was accustomed to holding my dad's head as his body shook uncontrollably in pain. Every week, we were in and out of hospitals, traveling to Indianapolis, Chicago and anywhere else that gave us hope for a cure.

It wasn't long before the cancer spread and he began to lose feeling in his left hand . . . then his arm . . . his left leg . . . his face . . . until half of his body no longer functioned and he was permanently bedridden. Ultimately, the doctors said it was only a matter of time, so my mom had him moved from the hospital to our home so we could spend his final few months together. We watched him slowly and painfully fight a battle that captured control of his body, diminished his mind, and eventually took his life. In his final moments on earth, I lay in his bed comforting him before watching him slip off to heaven.

At seven years old, I had already experienced life and death in a way many adults never do.

A New "Normal"

After my dad died, my mom, brother, and I were left to face

the sobering reality of life without him. We were all emotionally distraught by the fact that he was actually gone forever. For years, so much of our family's energies had been centered on the fight to keep my dad alive. We'd been able to hide our feelings behind the many distractions his care provided. Suddenly, we each had a world of emotions to confront, with nothing to distract us.

That haunting memory of my mother crying on the porch as my neighbor declared, "Go back where you came from," happened in the midst of this low point in our lives. Unfortunately, our neighbor wasn't the only one suggesting we leave the country. Several other people had told my mom the odds were against us and we'd be better off if she'd just take us back to Venezuela and start over.

Despite these comments, my mom decided to stay in the United States and fight to keep our family afloat. Though moving back to Venezuela would have made life easier on her, she refused to pull my brother and me out of the only life we had ever known right after the tragedy of losing our dad.

That loving and courageous decision came with a difficult downside: my mom needed to work a lot harder to keep our family financially afloat now that my dad's income was gone.

My mother spoke very broken English at the time, which severely limited her work options. The only jobs she could get required long, laborious hours. Mom was often exhausted from working such long hours and trying to deal with the pain of losing the love of her life. My brother, who was just starting middle school, was also trying to navigate becoming man of the house—all while being heartbroken and missing my dad. With two hurting people trying to lead our home, I was caught somewhere in the middle.

We were in turmoil as we struggled to figure out our new life. Explosive arguments were common in our home. My mother and brother fought through their emotions, expressing them loudly and vocally. Meanwhile, I quietly tried to hold my feelings in. But emotions always express themselves somehow, and at some point in middle school, I started hating everything about my life. It all felt so out of control, like there was nothing I could do to fix it. So I started taking out all my pain and frustration on the one thing I knew I could control: my body.

Before I knew it, I had become self-destructive.

For years, I struggled through fits of anorexia, bulimia, and cutting. I learned how to mask my feelings and emotions in front of others, knowing I would soon be able to release the pain once I was alone. I would also sneak out of the house late at night and go walking through the scariest parts of town, convinced that if I could become strong enough to ignore the fear of dark places, I would be strong enough to ignore the pain of what we were going through.

Though I was probably clinically depressed at the time, I was never diagnosed or treated because I didn't talk to anyone about it. Finally, after countless tear-soaked pillows and family blowups, I convinced myself that the world would be better off without me. One night after my mom and brother got into a huge fight and stormed out of the house, I was left by myself. The hurt and pain felt like too much to bear. So I came up with what I believed would be the easiest way to take my own life.

I tightly gripped the bottle of pills in my hand and began to unscrew the lid. I said a quick prayer: "Sorry, God; I can't do this anymore. Please forgive me . . ." And I began the final assault on my body.

Seconds before I reached the point of no return . . . the phone started ringing.

Scared Straight

I ignored the phone the first time, but it just kept ringing. I had no idea why anyone would be calling so incessantly at eleven o'clock on a school night, so I got up to check the Caller ID. It was my Aunt Tonna.

Worried that something had happened to my mom or brother, I answered the phone. Turns out she had called simply to talk and see how I was doing. She is someone I'd always looked up to, and since the two of us hadn't talked for a while, I decided to chat with her for a few minutes. I figured it would be my final good-bye.

Determined to complete my plan, I didn't tell her what was going on with me; I just tried to stick to small talk with her.

Before I knew it, though, we were laughing and making plans for the next time we would see each other.

Somehow she drew me out of the dark place I was in. We talked for two hours that night about absolutely nothing—and yet in that moment, it was *everything*. By the time I got off the phone, I had completely backed off the emotional ledge I'd been standing on. I *did* want to go on with my life.

The next day I woke up to the sun shining in my window, feeling happy about my conversation with Tonna and imagining how much fun we'd have the next time we hung out. Suddenly, like a punch to the stomach, I was gripped with fear as the enormity of what I had almost done came rushing back. I was terrified by just how crazy I had let myself get and the finality of the decision I'd almost made. I was barely a teenager, and I had nearly thrown everything away in one dark moment.

Waking up and realizing how far I had gone—and what my aunt had unknowingly rescued me from—scared me straight.

From that point on, I chose to fundamentally change my thinking. Suddenly I understood that if I'd followed through on my decision the night before, I not only would have taken my own life but also would have destroyed the lives of the people who loved me. I started realizing how many blessings I had and all the things I had to live for. I even allowed myself to believe that maybe God had a plan for my life after all.

I decided to abandon my patterns of self-abuse and begin

replacing them with positive ones. Instead of trying to hide from or numb my pain, I started journaling and confronting it head on. Instead of focusing on how bad I felt, I began helping other people who were struggling. Instead of walking through dark places to confront my fears, I signed up for sports and activities that challenged me to be genuinely fearless. Anytime I felt tempted to fall back into the patterns of self-destruction, I would fight to channel that energy into a positive activity. The change wasn't immediate or perfect, but slowly and surely I began setting the stage for a brighter future.

In the meantime, my mom realized that my brother and I had been seriously struggling. Convinced that our family wasn't recovering from our loss—and believing she could not help us if she was never around—she put in her two weeks' notice and quit her job. She then took her life savings and used them to turn our living room into a hair salon.

It really changed everything. We started learning to live and work together as a family again. Our home again became a place of happiness rather than a battleground. My mom became my brother's and my biggest cheerleader, encouraging and supporting us in finding things we loved to do. Most importantly, we began to heal emotionally and move through the loss of my father.

The one negative effect of my mom's decision to work from home, however, was that we soon fell below the poverty line. By the end of middle school, my brother and I were both working to help pay our family's expenses. We found full-time summer jobs working in the farmers' fields near our town. Though the work was hard, hot, and monotonous, we met really great people and found ways to make it fun. And even though finances were tight, things really started looking up. I can't say that life was easy, but for the first time since my dad died, I felt genuinely happy.

Figuring Out the Future

After my first day of high school, I came home and ecstatically told my mom every detail. We sat on the back porch, laughing about how I got lost after fifth period and barely made it to class on time. I talked about how excited I was about the next four years and all the fun things I wanted to do. Soon, though, Mom's expression changed, and her tone grew more serious.

"There's something I've been wanting to talk to you about," she began. Concerned, I sat up in my chair, listening intently. "It's about college," she said. "You have four years to figure out what you're going to do with your life because you're on your own financially after graduation."

Caught off guard by her bluntness, I sat back with a confused look on my face. I thought, *Why is she telling me this? To worry me? What can I do about it?*

As I was about to snap back, she said, "Kristina, I'm telling you this because I love you, and I believe in you. You are not meant to live in poverty your whole life, and I know that if you work hard, you can go to a great college and start fresh. *The choices you make right now will impact you for the rest of your life.*"

Mom went on to tell me what little she knew about the steps I could take to qualify for scholarships. We started brainstorming different ways I could get involved and begin building my qualifications as a scholarship applicant. A lot of her ideas seemed outlandish—like going to an expensive private school for free—but she had such faith in me that I started believing in the possibilities myself.

We talked about ideas for volunteering, how I could get better grades, and what to do to become a leader. When we ended that conversation, I felt incredibly motivated and ready to start moving!

That day was one of the most significant days of my life, because it was the first day I really began to believe I could accomplish big goals and do something meaningful with my life. My mom broke it down very simply for me: "If you work hard enough now to prove you are worthy of a scholarship, you can go to college for free." That simple but powerful statement stuck with me. As hard as my life had felt up until then, that conversation gave me hope and set a goal I could work toward.

Not Just for Top Students

I had always thought of a scholarship winner as someone who was supersmart and got perfect grades. As a student with only decent grades and average test scores, I had assumed that scholarships weren't for me. But after the conversation with my mom, I did a little research and discovered this was not the case—there were many ways to prove myself "scholarship worthy." I realized I could appeal to scholarship committees outside of academics and still have a chance of standing out. So I set out to find activities I could excel in.

At first, I wasn't successful in a lot of the things I tried. In fact, I fell on my face more times than I can count. I lost competitions I had prepared months for, was coldly rejected for positions I wanted very badly, and I learned I was very awkward in any sport that involved a ball. Each time I failed, however, I'd evaluate what I could do to improve my chances of succeeding the next time.

I also soon realized that while some of my peers had more natural talent than I did, I was willing to work harder and longer than most. On an average school day, I'd leave the house at 5:45 a.m. for a morning run and then get to school early for tutoring with my teachers. I'd return home around 9 p.m. after a sports practice, club meeting, and/or my job. After many late nights and hard work, I started to see some success: I won two Junior Olympics gold medals for gymnastics, raised enough money to travel to Haiti for missions work, and became one of the fastest runners in my high school.

One day in the spring of my freshman year, I got a letter in the mail saying that I had been selected to participate in Miss Indiana Junior Teen. I begged my mom to let me sign up. She said I could do it with the condition that I found a way to pay the $300 entrance fee myself, plus all other expenses.

I sold candy bars, knocked on doors asking for sponsorships, and held car washes to raise the money. The pageant organizers recommended hiring a coach to train with, but we couldn't afford one, so my mom and I spent hours going over the interview questions and other materials the pageant organization had sent us. My best friends surprised me the morning before I left, taking me out to breakfast to wish me luck. I told them to not get their hopes too high; I didn't think I even had a chance of making the semifinals.

When I got to the pageant in Indianapolis, my doubts were confirmed because 191 other girls had also been "selected" to participate in my age group. I felt a little tricked, but I decided that I had worked too hard to get there to quit now. *No point in getting discouraged and being stressed all weekend*, I thought. *I'll just give it my best effort and make sure I have fun.* And I did. Whether the other girls and I were about to compete, or starting dance parties in the hallway, I enjoyed myself.

On the final night of the competition, the judges narrowed the number of contestants from 191 to 40 semifinalists. Mine was the 38th name called. Ecstatic at making the Top 40, I was even more surprised and delighted when they announced me as the recipient of the Miss Congeniality title! Apparently, I had made a lot of friends during the weekend! That meant the world to me.

As we all nervously waited to hear the winner announced, I anticipated the final results as if I were a spectator. I had already given up any hope that I could win. In fact, I had predicted the winner and runners-up in my head.

The emcee started naming each runner-up, one by one. As the third runner-up, then the second and first were announced, I realized that the girls I thought would win had already been called to the front of the stage. I scanned up and down the rows, thinking through who else might be crowned. Suddenly I realized: *I could have a chance!*

My heart started racing at that small glimmer of hope as the emcee listed all the prizes the winner would receive and the experiences she would have in the coming year: an all-expenses-paid trip to Disney World for the national pageant, brand-new clothes, training with one of the top interview coaches, money, gifts, etc. Then came the announcement: "And the new winner of Miss Indiana Junior Teen is . . .

"Kristina Ellis!"

My jaw dropped, and I stood paralyzed for a moment.

My name! My name was called!

My mind was a swirl of thoughts: *What just happened? Did I hear them right? What's going on?*

Then I realized . . . *I have to move!*

I somehow walked to the front of the stage and accepted the award as my mom jumped chairs and raced to the stage, also in shock.

After the pageant, I was whisked into a life I could never have imagined. A few weeks after winning the title, I was flown to New York City, where I met the *Today* show cast, went on VIP tours, and stayed in luxury hotels. I'd worked so hard for everything up to that point in life, it felt incredible to sit back for once and be spoiled.

No More Cloud Nine

I came home from my trip to New York on cloud nine, still in disbelief at the experience I'd just had yet excited to share the craziness with my friends. I arrived at school just in time for lunch. At the time, I was friends with the "popular girls" and was hoping my Miss Indiana Junior Teen experience would help solidify my spot in the group.

Instead, I found my seat at the lunch table was missing. Figuring the girls didn't expect me to make it back in time, I just pulled up a chair. But as I sat down, not one girl looked up from her tray.

"Hi, everybody!" I said. "I'm so excited to see you!"

Still, I got no response. It was as if I weren't even there.

Ten minutes passed, and not one person said a word to me. I kept waiting to wake up from a weird dream or to finally catch on to some strange joke, but the bell rang and we were off to class.

I left the lunchroom with my mind racing, trying to figure out what I could have possibly done wrong to make my friends ignore me. As I walked the halls, I kept getting cold stares and dirty looks. At the end of the day, I begged someone to tell me what was going on.

The person finally admitted that a series of terrible rumors had been started about me, and they had taken off like wildfire throughout the school. Rumors like, "Kristina left town because she thought she was better than everyone else," and, "She hated all her friends and was just waiting for an opportunity to leave them."

Similar to the game of telephone, the rumors continually morphed from bad to worse as they were passed along. The worst part was that one of my cross-country teammates—someone I had been close friends with since the fourth grade—had started them.

My mom picked me up from school that day, still on a high from our trip. When I got into the car, she was smiling but I immediately burst into tears.

"I don't understand!" I sobbed.

"Oh, my goodness! What happened?" she asked.

"Everyone hates me now because of rumors that were started while we were gone! I have no clue what I did! They're not true!" I cried.

My mom tried to console me and encouraged me to call my teammate and get to the bottom of it. Once the girl was on the phone, I begged to know what she had said and why. She finally told me everything and admitted she had made up the lies. As she put it, "I wanted to hurt you because I thought you had become too good for me and were leaving me behind. You haven't been around in a few weeks, and I guess that scared me."

By the end of the conversation, she'd apologized several times, and I forgave her. Unfortunately, our reconciliation didn't stop the rumors from multiplying. I was called fake, fat, and a loser. People pulled chairs out from under me in the lunchroom, put threatening notes in my locker, and spat on me as I walked by. I spent many lunch periods eating alone in the bathroom and hiding my face in my locker as I wiped away tears.

Over the next month, I did everything I could to defend myself, but no one would listen. Eventually I learned to force a smile to hold back the tears, but inside, I was devastated and began to dread going to school.

One of the greatest moments of my life had become one of the most heartbreaking.

So many times I wished I could reverse time and never win the pageant title, just so I could have my friends back. Instead, I watched them walk away, and there was absolutely nothing I could do about it. Yet as painful as waking up and facing every day was . . . every day I got a little bit stronger.

Being so alienated taught me how to keep my head up and move on when I felt like I was being slapped in the face. It also made me even more driven to get into college. College became like a holy land to me; I thought if I just kept pushing through the hell I was in, I could make it to the other side.

By my junior year of high school, it didn't matter what mean things anyone said to me. I would not let their actions or their words sway me from my plans, my dreams . . . my future.

A Whole New World

The way I saw it, my senior year would determine where I would start the rest of my life as an adult. I could go to college and begin again anywhere in the world. So I sat down before the school year and wrote out a list of the goals I wanted to accomplish by graduation day:

1. Get full-ride funding for college
2. Get into a Top 20 university
3. Win Miss Indiana Teen USA
4. Build up my gymnastics team to 45 members
5. Win a cross-country team award

Under each goal I listed action steps I'd have to take to accomplish it. Step by step, I built my plans for getting into college, earning scholarships, and reaching my high school dreams. I read that list every single day that year.

As intimidating as the goals seemed, I realized I had nothing to lose by trying. Each day I made sure to work on the action steps. Throughout the year, I not only marked off the steps but also was able to achieve the goals. I built up my gymnastics team, my cross-country team won several notable awards, and I even won another pageant title: Miss Indiana Teen USA.

In the meantime, I spent every spare minute in the local college library trying to figure out the scholarship process.

Between school, sports, and work, I pulled several all-nighters. I read every book in the library on scholarships and interviewed everyone I could find who had useful information. I studied the stories of other students who found success in the scholarship application process, and I continually refined my strategy until I finally felt I had a formula for success. Then I took everything I had learned and used that to strategically fill out my scholarship applications, discovering some secrets along the way—secrets I'll share with you in this book.

The years of participating in sports and volunteering in the community . . . the countless hours spent in the library . . . the numerous awkward phone interviews . . . the hardships that ignited my determination—all of it was condensed onto a few sheets of paper. I poured my heart and emotions into each application. I obsessed over every detail, realizing that every scholarship dollar I received would be hours I wouldn't have to spend working in a fast-food restaurant in college. After months of work and hours of going over each application seemingly a hundred times, I finally placed the paperwork in the mail and hoped for the best.

I think the hardest part of the scholarship process was the

agonizing period of time between mailing off my applications and getting a response. I could hardly wait to hear back! When the first letter from a scholarship committee did arrive in the mail, I gathered my family around and excitedly tore it open. It was . . . a rejection letter. I threw it away, tried not to be disheartened, and continued to watch the mailbox.

I'm glad I didn't let that first rejection letter get me down, because things changed dramatically after that. One day, I got a big envelope in the mail informing me that I had made the first cut in the Coca-Cola Scholarship selection. Out of over 100,000 applicants, I was among the top 2,500 finalists. After a few additional application steps and flying to Coca-Cola's headquarters in Atlanta for an interview, I was selected as one of their National Scholars and received a $20,000 scholarship!

I was scared it might be a fluke until several other big envelopes containing acceptance letters arrived. Soon I had more money than I needed for college! After years of our family struggling with barely enough to get by, thousands and thousands of dollars in scholarship offers were suddenly right in front of me! I shed so many tears of happiness!

My ultimate scholarship dreams came true when I was contacted by the Bill & Melinda Gates Scholarship Foundation. I was informed I'd been selected as a recipient of their prestigious scholarship, which offered a full-ride to any school through my PhD! That is when it really hit me: I had made it to the other side!

With the Gates Scholarship, I was able to attend my dream school, Vanderbilt University, for free. It also fully funded my master's degree at Belmont University. I was blown away that any organization would want to invest so much in my future and would believe so much in my potential. Yet there are thousands of similar opportunities out there for you, being sponsored by other individuals or organizations.

Scholarships gave me the ability to completely devote myself to a college education and focus on building a new future. I'm proud to say that my brother was also able to go to college as a Gates Scholar and earn his master's degree in biomedical engineering.

We've both begun our dream careers and redefined our futures. Together we have proven that no matter what situation you're in, there is always a path to success.

You Can Too!

Over the past several years, the economy has taken a significant toll on many people's hopes and dreams. So many families with teenagers are struggling just to pay living expenses, let alone save for college! And while most high schoolers realize the impact a great education can have on their future, many don't believe there's any way they can afford it.

As you've read, I was one of those students. I felt so hopeless and intimidated by the thought of paying for college. Yet the work I put in to becoming scholarship worthy changed my life.

Now I want to help other students by sharing the strategies I discovered for success.

During the last few years, I've been on a mission to demystify the secrets that make students successful in the college-money game. I've had the opportunity to interview numerous scholarship administrators and financial-aid officers. I've also met with and interviewed several National Scholars who, like me, had tremendous success using little-known strategies that set them apart from the crowd. I've combined all of my research into this book, and now I'm giving you a solid platform from which to launch your efforts toward scholarship achievement. But rather than making you spend months trying to figure everything out, I've broken down all the details in a way you can understand quickly and simply.

My main goals are to help you see just how successful you can be with scholarships and to help you craft a strategy that sets you apart from all the other applicants trying to get scholarships each year. By the end of this book, you will be prepared to chart your own course to earning free money for college!

2

THE FOUNDATION

Better You = Better Application

The choices you make right now will impact you for the rest of your life.

My mother's statement kept echoing in my head throughout my senior year of high school. While I was in the library at night applying for scholarships and sorting through piles of paper, I had moments of frustration and times when I wondered, *Why am I working so hard? Is it really going to make a difference?* When my boyfriend or my circle of friends would ask me to go out with them, I had to keep repeating that sentence over and over in my head, reminding myself that my extra efforts would eventually pay off.

They weren't easy choices, but I could imagine what going to college for free could do for my life. Skipping a few high school parties and working a little longer into the night would do a lot to determine where I would spend the rest of my life, what my career options would be, and the amount of financial stress I would face as an adult. I really wanted to go to college, but without scholarships or a financial miracle, I'd either have to settle for less than my dreams or end up with massive amounts of debt.

Nobody else was in control of my life. Nobody else would suffer the consequences of my decisions but me. Fortunately, I had a mother who realized the potential I had to launch myself forward at that crucial time—and she passed that confidence on to me. But whether or not I ran with it was up to me.

Maybe you don't have someone in your life who is casting a vision for you. If you don't, let me be that person. I'm here as living proof to tell you: if you are in high school right now, this is your moment to choose.

The Turning Point

Up to this moment, you may have felt it was your teachers and parents who were driving your success: you go to school, make good grades, and do what you're supposed to do to make them happy. But now is the turning point. **Now is when you determine what YOUR goals are. Now is when you decide how far you are willing to go to make YOUR dreams happen.** Your parents and other caring adults can help, and they can be wonderful assets to you, but ultimately YOU have to guide your own ship and drive things forward to enjoy significant scholarship success.

You are at a prime age. Your whole life is ahead of you, and you can plan what you want to do with it. Incredible things can happen when a teenager makes a decision to wholeheartedly move forward with his or her goals. So think long and hard about what you want out of life.

I encourage you to *dream big* but also to realize that hard work and perseverance come with the package. It takes effort to reach those dreams. But I can promise you, the effort is worth it!

This is your time! Have fun with it and make incredible memories. Learn, grow, and challenge yourself. Be focused, determined, and prepared for success. And remember . . . *The choices you make right now will impact you for the rest of your life.*

Laying the Foundation

Four basic qualities create the foundation for any student to achieve scholarship success: fearlessness, drive, discipline, and following direction.

FEARLESSNESS

What is fearlessness? Does it mean that you're never afraid, never have doubts, or never worry? Absolutely not. Taylor Swift described it wonderfully in the liner notes of her *Fearless* album: "To me, Fearless is not the absence of fear. It's not being completely unafraid. To me, Fearless is having fears. Fearless is having doubts. Lots of them. To me, Fearless is living in spite of those things that scare you to death."

I've found this quality evident in all the major scholarship winners I've talked with. Their passion and burning desire to find success far surpassed any fears or doubts they had. Now, that doesn't mean they were never scared. It just means they were able to reach deep down within to find the courage to tackle any fear or doubt that tried to hold them back.

Applying for scholarships requires you to risk putting yourself out there. You may get rejected and walk away empty-handed, and I'll be the first to admit that the thought ran through my head multiple times. But if you don't put yourself out there, you won't win. So give yourself a chance! Put yourself in a position to succeed! As past *American Idol* finalist Melinda Doolittle's mother always told her, sometimes we just have to "do it afraid." When we do that and push through our fears, willingly committing to the process even though we know we might be disappointed, we become fearless.

What kinds of things fuel fearlessness?

I believe the first thing that fuels fearlessness is *faith*. Faith is moving forward *anyway*, trusting that things will work. There is no guarantee you will win, but you massively increase your chances when you are willing to wholeheartedly take the risk and put forth your best effort, all the while believing for the best.

The second important thing is *commitment*—determining to stick with the process, regardless of how difficult it becomes. Even when fears arise, your commitment is what makes you stay on course.

A lot of people win scholarships just because they tried. Students are often shocked to learn that numerous scholarship awards go unclaimed each year because no one applied for them! Rather than focusing on a few big scholarships and giving up if you don't win, *keep believing* and *keep trying*! Sometimes that's all it takes to win scholarships worth a *lot* of money!

DRIVE

Drive is the urgency to move forward. It is a desire that motivates you to reach for a goal. True drive is when you're relentlessly determined to work hard, push through any challenges, and do *whatever it takes* because the end goal is so valuable to you.

Drive is what propels major scholarship winners to succeed. Drive is what carries them through long days of school, work, sports, clubs, and community service. And it's what will move *you* to try to excel in everything you do:

- to work hard in your activities
- to challenge yourself to get the best grades you can
- to go above and beyond your normal school day and spend extra hours in the scholarship pursuit.

My senior year was one of the busiest years of my life. In addition to my Miss Indiana Teen USA activities, I ran on the cross-country team, coached a gymnastics team of 45 girls, was in several clubs, was active in my church's youth group . . . and then I also had scholarships to apply for. While my mom was extremely supportive, the choice to work hard and push through was mine and mine alone. Somewhere along the way, I realized that no amount of cheering, support, or help from Mom could carry me through to the end if I didn't make the choice to strive for my own positive future.

When you choose to be "all in"—with scholarships or anything else you've set your mind to do—your drive helps push you across the finish line.

DISCIPLINE

While drive is what keeps you going, *discipline* is what keeps you on track. Discipline is learning to exercise self-control and dedication. It is saying no to distractions and saying yes to taking the necessary steps to reach a goal. My pastor, Danny Chambers, described it so well when he said, "Discipline is nothing more than creating the habit of doing what you don't want to do so that you can be who you want to be and have what you want to have in life."

To properly balance every area of preparation in the scholarship process takes discipline. I can guarantee there will be moments where you absolutely don't feel like working on things that will help you prepare for your future. Discipline comes into play when all your friends are out having fun but you stay home to work on an application that is due the next day. Being disciplined may mean you give up watching your favorite TV show for a few weeks, cut out time on Facebook, stick to a specific schedule, and sometimes work when you're tired. It is forcing yourself to do what you should to reach your goal.

Why not view this process as the most important—and best-paying—part-time job you'll ever have? Think of it: for spending perhaps 15 total hours in research, planning, writing, and processing paperwork for the Coca-Cola Scholarship, my "wages" came out to over $1,300 per hour! Even if you only spend three hours putting together an application for a $1,000 scholarship, that's still $333 per hour if you win! A little discipline can really pay off!

By practicing discipline and taking the necessary steps even when you don't want to, you will greatly increase your chances for scholarship success.

FOLLOWING DIRECTION

The final part of building your foundation is following direction. For most every adventure in life, a road map exists to guide you to your destination, developed by people who have successfully traveled the path before you. They've already learned the tricks to navigating the twists and turns of the journey; they've discovered the secrets to arriving at your intended location safely and on time. All you have to do is follow the directions.

Yet, especially in the area of scholarships, students often

don't even know that a map exists! They and their parents stumble through the financial aspects of college, only figuring out the right directions after it's too late—after they've wandered in circles and wasted a lot of time and energy. Unfortunately, those unnecessary detours can also cost them money.

Another problem that can affect your progress is trying to take shortcuts—either skipping steps or giving only a halfhearted effort. Plenty of students with big dreams want to get to the fun part without getting a little dirty on the trails or climbing the hills it often takes to get there. They think, *Do I really need to take those classes?* Or, *It doesn't really matter if I step up for a leadership position.* Or, *I don't want to bother having someone else proofread my essays.* Yet avoiding those small, sometimes boring trail markers can derail the big dream.

In this book, I have laid out a step-by-step map to lead you through the scholarship application process. These are steps that both scholarship winners and scholarship experts agree can make a huge difference.

Following the directions of the people who were successful before me made a huge difference in my scholarship pursuit. I didn't know anything about this world of "free money for college" when I first started my journey. But through research, I was able to find great information and advice from others who had successfully preceded me in the process—as well as those who were on the organizational side (the scholarship and financial-aid experts). Could I have gotten lucky and figured it out on my own? Maybe . . . but why guess when proven routes to success are available?

I encourage you to use the well-traveled directions in this book to guide you through the process.

One Thing at a Time

These four qualities—fearlessness, drive, discipline, and following direction—will help you lay the foundation for success. Even if you don't think you possess all of these qualities now, you can develop them. They are something anyone can do!

Just take it one day at a time. Don't stress or worry about trying to figure it out overnight. **Ask yourself each morning,** *What can I do today to improve and take a step forward in laying my foundation?* If you've always wanted to audition for a school musical but have been too nervous in the past, commit to being fearless and trying it this year. If you are usually late turning in your homework, start practicing daily discipline by committing to turn in your next assignment on time.

Put these four qualities on a sticky note and post them where you'll see them every day—your locker, the dashboard of your car, your bathroom mirror, or your closet door. When you see the qualities, ask yourself if you are practicing each one and consider how you can improve. Soon these qualities will start to become second nature—and ultimately they'll become part of how you approach life, which can help you far beyond your scholarship search.

Plan Early

Don't make the error that a lot of students make: assuming, "Because I'm a freshman, I don't need to start thinking about scholarship applications."

That couldn't be further from the truth. Many scholarships judge you based on your entire high school experience. The sooner you start preparing for the scholarship process, the better—especially because, according to Dan Toplitt at Scholarship Strategies, 90 percent of scholarship seekers are in their junior year or later before they take the first step.

Becoming aware of the things you can do *right now* to set yourself apart from the crowd gives you:

- a head start on the majority of scholarship seekers, and
- the ability to create a strategic success plan for high school.

If you start planning too late, you may miss out on the needed courses, leadership experiences, and volunteer opportunities that could really help you stand out for major scholarships. **You should start preparing and applying for scholarships as soon as college becomes a serious goal for you.** I'll walk you through the steps in that process in the following chapters. Stick with me. We'll get there together!

▶ Now is the time to take responsibility for your future. It's up to you to *determine your goals* and how far you're willing to go to make them happen.

▶ Four qualities *lay the foundation* for scholarship success: fearlessness, drive, discipline, and following direction.

▶ *Start planning early* to get a head start on scholarship success.

ACTION STEPS

○ Cast a vision for your life. Write down your long-term goals and what you plan on doing to achieve them.

○ Write down what you can do to improve within each of the four qualities of laying the foundation for scholarship success: fearlessness, drive, discipline, and following direction. Read and work on applying that foundation every day for a month, until the qualities become part of who you are.

3

SHOW ME THE MONEY

Understanding College Financing

A recent College Board study reports that the average cost of attending a public four-year university is more than $21,000 per year while a private four-year university is double that amount. According to the US Census Bureau's American Community Survey, those figures have been increasing at a rate of approximately 5.5 percent per year; meanwhile, the median family income has decreased by more than 7 percent in the past three years. Truly, college isn't cheap!

Maybe you and your family have seen the numbers and you're tempted to wave the white flag of surrender. I can't say that I blame you. Thinking through how to pay for college can feel completely overwhelming! To make matters worse, understanding what help and financial aid are available can be confusing. There are all those forms and abbreviations and unfamiliar words (FAFSA, CSS profile, different types of loans and grants, work-study, and on and on). Additionally, each college has its own way of determining who gets how much financial assistance. Navigating the financial-aid maze can be a challenge.

Thankfully, most families don't pay full price for college. In 2010–11, according to the College Board's *Trends in Higher Education*, full-time undergrads received an average of $12,455 in financial aid. This figure doesn't even include scholarship money! So if you take the time to understand how the financial-aid system works, it can yield big rewards.

While this book is primarily focused on helping you win scholarships, it is important that you first understand the basics of college financing. I will outline the big picture of the financial-aid system for you in this chapter. When we're finished, you'll be even more confident that affording a great college education is within your reach.

Playing by the Rules

Think of financial aid as the rules of a game. Once you learn how all the pieces and parts fit together, you can play to win. The good news is, the prizes for winning are much greater than in any game you've ever played. By learning to play by the rules, I received over half a million dollars in free money for college! Now it's time for you to get *your* share. To begin, you need to consider how much you need.

Paying several thousand dollars each year for college isn't easy for the majority of families. Most families need help making college affordable. The government and the schools themselves offer some students help with paying for college based on their financial need.

To determine your need, the US Department of Education will have you fill out the FAFSA (Free Application for Federal Student Aid) form prior to your first year of college. This form asks a lot of questions about your family's finances, including how much you and your parents earn, and what kind of assets you have. This information is then plugged into the department's formula to generate your expected family contribution, or EFC. The EFC is the amount of money the government believes your family should be able to contribute toward your college education. Visit FAFSA.ed.gov and use the FAFSA4caster tool to get an idea of what your EFC will be.

Filling out the FAFSA takes a little time, but it is an essential part of the college-funding process for most families. Once you have completed the FAFSA, you will have a clearer understanding of how much money you'll need for college.

Leaving Your Options Open

Students sometimes make the mistake of not applying for financial aid because they believe their family makes too much money to qualify for assistance when, in fact, families with more than $150,000 in annual income can qualify for financial assistance!

While it's not all "free" money (you may be offered low-interest loans), you want to make sure you have as many options available as possible. And applying for financial aid makes that happen.

It never hurts to try. Especially since, according to the National Center for Education, over two-thirds of college students accept some form of financial aid each year. Applying for assistance can only help, and you may actually be pleasantly surprised.

When filling out the FAFSA, you will be asked to identify which colleges you are considering and would like your paperwork sent to. The information from this form is sent to the schools' financial-aid departments, which use your FAFSA-generated EFC (expected family contribution) to create a financial-aid package. This package details the financial assistance each school, and the government, can offer you based on the school's cost of attendance, or COA. The COA is the total amount it costs to go to the school, including tuition, fees, room and board, books, and other expenses. The options in the package come from a variety of places, including loans, grants, work-study programs, and scholarships.

A lot of students mistakenly think they could never afford a top private school education and immediately limit their college search to public and community colleges in their price range.

They don't realize the incredible amount of financial aid that some of the top institutions provide.

If you have prepared yourself to be admitted to a university and have demonstrated significant financial need (as determined by your EFC), many private colleges and universities have the endowments and funding to meet your need. **Because of additional grants and gift aid these schools typically offer, it can be cheaper for needy students to go to an expensive private university than a public university.** For example, you may be offered only government grants and loans at the public university, whereas the private university may have more private grants and gift aid to give away.

Some top universities, in seeking to attract the best and brightest students, have actually implemented no-loan financial-need policies, meaning that if you get accepted into that school, it foots the bill and helps pay for anything outside of your expected family contribution. So if your EFC says your family can contribute $5,000 and the school costs $45,000, the school itself may make up the $40,000 difference with gift aid.

Elements That Make Up the Financial-Aid Package

The financial-aid package presented to you will vary depending on the school. It is important to distinguish between gift aid and loan money that has to be paid back. Don't assume that the final amount of aid a school is offering you comes without a cost. Loans have to be paid back, and work-study programs require you to work on campus for the money promised.

It's easy to fall for the appeal of a college sales pitch, so it's all the more important to look at each piece of your personal financial-aid package at each school and determine the best fit for you.

Let's discuss what each element of the package means. Typically those elements are scholarships and grants, student loans, and work-study programs.

SCHOLARSHIPS AND GRANTS

The terms *scholarship* and *grant* are often used interchangeably as they both describe money that is gifted to a student with no expectation of repayment. Most grants are given to students based on their financial need as determined by their FAFSA application. Scholarships derive from a variety of sources. Some are awarded simply as a result of the information you shared in your admissions application. Others take a bit more work, requiring additional applications, essays, and interviews. As I hope you understand already, the small investment of time you put into applying for scholarships can be well worth it, yielding hundreds of thousands of dollars you don't have to pay back! This is clearly the most attractive form of financial aid, and it is the focus of this book.

STUDENT LOANS

A student loan is money you can borrow for college that has to be repaid with interest. This means you not only have to pay back the entire amount of money you borrowed but also an additional percentage of the loan that compounds each year. By the time you pay it all back, the total loan amount can be much larger than the amount you originally borrowed.

I'll never forget those college admissions officers at some of the expensive schools I visited who tried to convince me that taking out student loans was "no big deal." They told me their educational program was far more valuable than the massive amount of debt I would assume and that I would easily be able to pay off the debt with the fantastic job I would get because of their school's degree.

Let me tell you now that student loans stink! Once you graduate, they are like haunting creatures that don't go away and that suck the joy out of your newfound success. Avoid them by all means possible!

That being said, though, sometimes loans are necessary evils and the best options you have to move forward.

Loans for college come in two forms: subsidized and unsubsidized. Subsidized loans are need-based loans that offer an extra benefit to the borrower, such as deferred interest payments while in college; that means while you are in school, the government or another group pays the interest. For example, with the Direct

Stafford Loan, the government pays a student's interest payments while he or she is in school and for six months after. Unsubsidized loans, on the other hand, are available to students and families regardless of financial need. With these loans, however, interest often begins accumulating the moment a student signs for the loan. Most college loan repayment plans start within a few months of graduation or once you are no longer attending school.

It is important to note the little-known but critical fact that student loan debt doesn't go away until it is paid off. Even if you declare bankruptcy, you (or whoever co-signed the loan agreement with you) are still responsible for repayment. Until you have taken out significant amounts of student loans and experienced their long-term effect, it can be hard to understand just how miserable they are to pay back. If you find yourself in a position where taking out massive student loans is your only option for attending that expensive school you've dreamed of, you may want to consider a more affordable school.

Let me give you an example of just how inconvenient loans can be to pay off in the long-term:

Let's say your dream school is the University of Notre Dame, where the estimated cost of attendance (COA) at the time of this writing is $57,805 per year. The average starting salary of a Notre Dame graduate is $52,900. That would put your monthly income at $4,408. After taxes, it would be $3,282. Using current estimates, let's put that into a budget:

Monthly Salary After Taxes	$3,282.92
Rent/ Mortgage	$1,100
Home/ Rental, Health, and Dental Insurance	$153
Electricity	$60
Gas (Utilities)	$50
Water	$20
Trash	$15
Phone	$80
Cable	$35
Internet	$35
Food	$300
Shopping	$100
Entertainment	$75
Savings	$100
Car Payment	$250
Insurance	$50
Gas/ Fuel	$150
TOTAL	$2,573
Amount Left	*$709*

With the modest projections listed here, you would have only $709 total, or $164 per week, left to spend outside of your budget. That doesn't include gym memberships, travel, or the bridesmaid dress you need to buy for your best friend's wedding. Then come the student loans . . .

With the average cost of attendance being $57,805 per year, the total cost of a four-year degree comes to $231,220. Let's say you get grants and scholarships to pay for over half of that amount and decide to take out $25,000 per year in student loans (or $100,000 over the course of your education). If you accept a federal Stafford Loan with a set interest rate of 6.8 percent, your financial picture would look like this:

STUDENT LOAN

Student Loan	$100,000
Interest Rate	6.8%
Loan Term	10 years
MONTHLY LOAN PAYMENT	$1,150.80

MONTHLY BUDGET OVERVIEW

Monthly Salary Amount	$3,282.92
Monthly Budget Costs	$2,573.00
Monthly Loan Payments	$1,150.80
WHAT'S LEFT	- $ 440.88

What this means is that in this very common scenario, even if you get that "great" job after college and you take out student loans for less than half the cost of attending Notre Dame, you still would not be able to pay your bills after graduation. Actually, you could fall $440 short of paying your bills each month!

That is the hard truth about student loans. They seem so simple before you start college, but as you dig deeper, you realize how complicated they can make your financial picture later in life. Choose wisely, and evaluate the costs and benefits before taking out a student loan.

Students demonstrating financial need are often offered a work-study option as part of their financial-aid package. Work-study is basically a guaranteed part-time job at the school or at a federal, state, or local public agency, a private nonprofit organization, or a private for-profit organization. Students work during the school year, earning up to the fixed amount of money stated in their financial-aid award letter.

The Financial-Aid Office

One of the first college offices most families come into contact with is financial aid. This office not only manages financial assistance for students but also plays a very important role in the scholarship process. Its staff acts as the liaison between you and any financial organization that will be disbursing funds for your education, including scholarship programs.

Make a point to become good friends with the financial-aid officer (FAO) you are assigned to, as that person will organize all of your assistance, including scholarships, grants, loans, and work-study. FAOs communicate with your scholarship programs as needed and insure that your money goes to the right place at the right time.

Your financial-aid officer can act as both an advocate and a gatekeeper. For example, one of my scholarship programs offered to pay for a laptop if it was considered part of my school's official cost of attendance. My university didn't typically include laptops in that calculation, but my financial-aid officer modified my COA to include a laptop expense, and within a few weeks, my scholarship program sent money for the computer. If it weren't for my FAO going above and beyond, that would not have been possible.

Your Aid Package

Once accepted into a university, you will receive a letter from the school's financial-aid office with your award package. When evaluating various packages—and before finally deciding which school to attend—be sure to talk to an FAO at each school regarding how your outside scholarship winnings will impact your overall aid package. Clarifying your ultimate costs after outside scholarships have been factored in can help shape your decision about where to go to school.

Understanding your financial-aid award package is critical. **As you receive scholarships, monitor and confirm that all the funds land in the right place. Failing to stay on top of this one area can cost your family thousands of dollars without ever knowing it.**

I gently battled several times with my financial-aid officers about small errors in my package. For example, in my freshman year of college, a computer error caused $1,500 to disappear from one of my scholarships and be replaced with a loan. Initially, my FAO didn't agree that there was an error. But because I had studied and understood every element of my package, I was able to explain it to her effectively, and the school reinstated the scholarship money into my account.

The financial-aid department at each school deals with hundreds, if not tens of thousands, of students every year and juggles millions of dollars. Mistakes can be made. Be smart, be vigilant, and of course, always be nice.

Cash in Your Pocket

Scholarships can pay for more than just tuition expenses. Each university has an official cost of attendance that includes housing, food, transportation, books, and personal expenses—which scholarships can be used to cover. Students are often surprised to learn that my university cut me a check for around $9,000 per semester to spend on books and living expenses once I lived off campus. When I lived in the dorms and was on the meal plan, I'd still get a few thousand dollars a year as a result of having enough scholarship money to cover the designated personal expenses in the cost of attendance. Use this as motivation to get as many scholarships as possible. Extra scholarships can eventually mean extra cash in your pocket.

Intelligent Spending in College

Loan companies often view college students as vulnerable prey. They'll try to sell you on loans, credit cards, or whatever it takes to help you get that college experience with seemingly no money upfront. However, by the time your school bills are in hand, those people are long gone.

While I do hope you get to have a carefree college experience, I also don't want you or your parents to have a stressful start to your post-college adult life. **Evaluate the long-term effects that each financial decision will have on your life before you jump in.** Brainstorm ways you can reach your goals and dreams without the hefty price tag.

Let's say you have your heart set on attending Harvard because its name has power on a resume. But Harvard costs more than $50,000 a year, and it offers you less than $10,000 in aid. After four years at Harvard, you could have over $160,000 in debt. In that situation, it is wise to consider alternative college solutions that will still set you up for your career goals without drowning you in debt.

Maybe you want to be a book editor. In that case, interning and developing relationships at a major publishing company while attending a more affordable university could open similar doors and put you in competition with Harvard students. Without the obligation of paying back all that debt, you may have more time to gain credentials that will help you compete in the real world.

Think creatively about ways to maximize your resume while keeping money in your pocket. I long for you to earn a full-ride scholarship to your dream school after reading and applying the principles in this book. But if you don't get it all paid for, I still want you to graduate as debt-free as possible.

● ●

For more information and resources on strategies for financing your education, visit my website, TheCollegeNinja.com.

● ●

SUMMARY POINTS

▶ *The FAFSA* is used to determine what your family is expected to contribute to your college education, as well as what government and school financial aid you're eligible for.

▶ *Financial-aid packages* are composed of scholarships and grants, student loans, and work-study programs.

▶ *While student loans* can be a useful element to funding your education, use caution when deciding if they're right for you and how much is truly needed.

▶ Always be on your best behavior when speaking with *financial-aid officers.* These individuals are typically super-helpful resources who can provide you with significant assistance in the scholarship process.

ACTION STEPS

○ Visit FAFSA.ed.gov and utilize the FAFSA4caster tool to get an idea of the financial-aid package you might receive.

O Start gathering your previous years' financial data to use in filling out your FAFSA. For most people, tax forms and bank statements will suffice.

O Visit the financial-aid websites for the schools you want to apply to. Get a feel for the schools' cost of attendance and financial-aid process. Make sure to take note of any deadlines.

4

SCHOLARSHIP SNAPSHOT

An Overview of the Basics

I t should be pretty obvious by now that free money—both scholarships and grants—is the best way to pay for college. Literally thousands of scholarships are awarded each year equaling millions of dollars being given away to help with college expenses. With determination and the right preparation, there is no reason why some of that money can't be yours!

So many students give up on themselves and their chances of winning scholarships before they even try. They assume—wrongly—that they could never have a shot because:

- They aren't smart enough.
- They don't come from the right background.
- They don't have some enormous talent.
- They aren't that lucky.

Yet over and over again, I've seen what initially appear to be the most unlikely candidates walk away from the scholarship process with the most money.

Students who have struggled with dyslexia, ADHD, troubles in school, abuse, divorce, and poverty have not only gone on to win full scholarships for college but also successfully completed college at the top of their class. These students often know they are entering the application process at a disadvantage, and their situation motivates them to commit to working harder than everyone else. They also learn to focus on the things they *can* do. **If you are determined to work harder, smarter, and more strategically than everyone else, there is almost no setback or mistake you can't overcome.**

Very rarely do major scholarship winners just stumble their way into success. Most of them will tell you they put an extraordinary amount of effort into creating and executing a strategy to help them stand out. Before you can develop a winning personal strategy, you first need to understand the basics of scholarships.

In this chapter, I will explain the main types of scholarships, how to find scholarships, and the essentials of the scholarship application. First, though, make a commitment to yourself to give the scholarship quest your best effort. As you learn about scholarship basics, read with the thought of how you will personally use this information to your benefit. I promise you, the results can change your life!

Not All Scholarships Are the Same

The biggest distinction between scholarships is need-based

versus merit-based. Need-based scholarships factor in a family's financial status to determine if a student is eligible to receive the award. Some scholarships and grants are given solely on the basis of financial need. For example, many states and schools have grants and scholarships that go to all students within a certain financial bracket who meet basic academic criteria.

For students who do not meet the need-based criteria, there is the wonderful world of merit-based scholarships. *Merit* is conduct or character that deserves honor or reward. In other words, merit-based scholarships are awarded because of a student's accomplishments, ability, involvement, background, unique traits, or potential.

Every **future college student is a candidate for merit-based scholarships!** Universities, organizations, private donors, and corporate sponsors give merit-based scholarships for almost anything you can think of—for being the son or daughter of an alum, for being a minority, for community service, and much more (see sidebar). Regardless of your background and experience, if you dig deep enough, you'll find scholarships that match who you are!

They Give Scholarships for *That*?

Here are some strange but interesting scholarship qualifiers. And no, I'm not making these up!

1. Being exceptionally tall
2. Being exceptionally short
3. Loving to vacuum
4. Bagpiping skills
5. Being an organ donor
6. Having a zombie-apocalypse escape plan
7. Duck-calling
8. Being left-handed
9. Having knowledge about fire sprinklers
10. Being a skateboarder

Beginning Your Search

When I talk with people about the scholarships I received, I often hear, "You're so lucky." While I have been very fortunate to be honored by some of the top scholarship programs in the country, it is important to understand that I also received my share of painful rejection letters. Only after high school did I realize how well I had done in the scholarship process, because while I won more money than I needed, I was also turned down for some scholarships I really wanted and worked hard to win. But I still won plenty of college funding because I used a proven method of applying for scholarships: *cast wide* and *go deep*.

CAST WIDE

One of the secrets to my success was to cast my net far and wide. This tactic allowed me to pull in several big fish I never would have caught with just a single line. It also meant if I lost a fish (was rejected by a scholarship), I still had others to take its place.

In applying for a scholarship, you are selling yourself on a piece of paper. One scholarship committee could be completely blown away with your application while another could pass over the exact same application. **The more scholarships you apply to, the more chances you have of being selected for one.** So don't put all your eggs in one basket. Spread your efforts wide to increase the odds of success.

I was watching a crime show the other day in which the police were interrogating a goofy-looking "ladies' man." The cops wanted to know how someone who was socially awkward and not very attractive always ended up with the most beautiful women. He explained to the detectives that it's a numbers game: yes, he always had a beautiful lady by his side, but to get that one lady he endured rejection by the 20 other beautiful ladies he had asked out before her.

I like to call that numbers game "the multiplicity rule": the more you put yourself out there, the greater your chances of success. Still, I recommend that you decide on a few key scholarships you want the most—and focus extra effort on them.

GO DEEP

As mentioned earlier in this chapter, thousands of scholarships are given out each year. Since you can't possibly apply for them all, it's important to find the ones that fit you best, even as you are casting your net wide. **It is better to put your strongest effort into a few scholarships that fit you well than to waste weak efforts on numerous scholarships that may not suit you at all.** When it comes to applying for scholarships, *quality* should trump *quantity.*

Your search can be as broad or as narrow as you choose. There are scholarship programs that receive more than 100,000 applicants each year and have very few stipulations regarding who can apply. In contrast, there are also some very restricted scholarship programs that limit who can apply: for example, if you are Catholic and have the last name Zolp (an actual scholarship for students attending one university in Chicago). Reflect on who you are and what you want, determine your college goals, and then go after the scholarships that fit you best. These "best fits" are your strongest investments in your future—the ones on which you should spend most of your time and energy.

Scholarship Resources

Many resources are available to help you find scholarships. With just a few hours of searching, you can develop a solid list of scholarships that could send you down the road to collegiate financial freedom.

Although it can be tempting to apply to the first scholarships you come across, instead focus your time on the ones you have the greatest chance of winning. Use the resources outlined here to find the most fitting scholarships *for you.*

BOOKS

Every year, a few authors go to tremendous efforts to bring you massive books full of current scholarship listings. They organize and itemize the specific criteria that can help you find scholarships that match you. Books such as *The Ultimate Scholarship Book* by Gen Tanabe and *Kaplan Scholarships* by Kaplan are packed with information that could bring in thousands of dollars for you!

ONLINE SCHOLARSHIP DATABASES

Online databases such as Fastweb.com and Scholarships.com help narrow the search for you. After you type in information about yourself, scholarship results are generated that match your background, interests, and attributes. Most of the databases provide detailed information about scholarship programs and link to each program's application. But a downfall of these resources is that you literally don't know what you're missing, because the database doesn't always match you with every scholarship you are actually eligible for.

In contrast, when you use scholarship books you can see all the scholarships available and determine your eligibility for yourself. I strongly recommend using a combination of online resources *and* books.

Conducting your own Google search can also be a relatively effective way to find scholarships. Typing in strong keywords that match your characteristics, such as "athletic scholarship," "science scholarship," or "leadership scholarship," can often link you to surprisingly well-matched results.

● ●

For more guidance, links, and resources, visit www.TheCollegeNinja.com.

● ●

YOUR HIGH SCHOOL

Most high schools have scholarship resources available to their students. One of the most effective contact people for many students is their guidance counselor, the point person for scholarship programs seeking to reach students at your school. Guidance counselors can usually provide you with the right contacts and resources.

Also, be on the lookout for flyers and listen for school announcements regarding what's available.

Alumni from your high school can be a great resource too. Ask your guidance counselor or teachers for names of students who won significant amounts of scholarship money in previous years. Reach out to those alumni via e-mail or social media and ask if they'd be willing to share some of their keys to success.

More often than not, these past students are excited to let up-and-coming scholarship seekers in on their strategies. They may even agree to help review some of your applications, which would be a major bonus!

COLLEGES AND UNIVERSITIES

Most universities give a variety of their own merit- and need-based scholarships. Once you decide on your top prospective schools, search their websites for the scholarships they provide.

Often, universities have separate applications for admissions and for their merit-based scholarships. Many of these merit-based scholarship applications are due around the same time the college application is due—and well before you find out if you're admitted—so don't procrastinate. For example, the application for Vanderbilt's Ingram Scholars Program, which offers students a four-year, full-tuition scholarship (tuition is $40,320 per year) plus volunteer service stipends, is due on December 1, more than a month before the admissions application deadline and four months before university acceptance letters are officially mailed. Be aware of these important deadlines so you don't miss out on the opportunity for large scholarships offered by your future school!

YOUR COMMUNITY

Civic organizations, such as the Rotary Club and the Elks Foundation, give back to their communities by helping local students go to college. Even some churches or church denominations offer college scholarships. Survey your community and region to see who sponsors scholarships.

Your school guidance counselor will often have this information, but if you are having trouble finding definitive answers, don't hesitate to pick up the phone and ask an organization directly if it offers scholarships.

The Scholarship Application

A scholarship application is the key—the gateway—to tens of thousands of dollars. Yes, I mean those thin sheets of 8½˝ x 11˝ paper that fit into a manila envelope. They unlock the door that leads to thousands of dollars.

Crazy, huh?

Most students just slap together their application like any other form, not realizing the importance of each component. But I'm here to teach you the skill and thought that goes into WINNING applications. By thinking through each part of the application form ahead of time, you can make a big difference in your scholarship success.

The application form varies from program to program, but most scholarships require students to respond to key components. The following is a brief overview of the most common components scholarship programs use to evaluate applicants. I'll go into more detail about strategies for each area later in the

book, but this will help you begin to understand the most important pieces of the scholarship puzzle.

ACADEMICS

Most scholarship programs require students to report their
grade point average (GPA). Some have students submit their
transcripts—an overview of their high school coursework and
grades—for verification. Scholarship programs often have a
minimum GPA cutoff, varying in increments of .25 on a 4.0 scale
(2.75, 3.0, etc.). Some scholarship programs require students
to submit their standardized test scores as well. Don't worry if
you're not proud of your scores. You can still experience great
scholarship success. In chapter 5, I'll share more details to help
you prepare for academic requirements.

EXTRACURRICULAR ACTIVITIES

Another key component of the scholarship application is an
evaluation of your extracurricular activities—or how you spend
your time outside of class. Scholarship committees want to see
that you are a meaningful part of your community and a generally well-rounded person. If your priorities are partying, cruising
around, and watching hours of TV, you are probably not the best
candidate for a scholarship.

Some key ways to demonstrate your extracurricular involvement are through athletics, volunteer work, club membership,

and employment. Certain scholarship programs ask specifics such as, "Where have you been employed over the past four years?" or "What clubs have you been affiliated with while in high school?" A commitment to staying active and involved is an attractive characteristic in an applicant. In chapter 5, I discuss creative ways to show the judges how your participation in activities makes you an excellent candidate for their scholarship.

HONORS AND AWARDS

Being asked to list past honors and awards gives applicants a chance to show the results of their efforts in high school. From winning your conference championship in track to making honor roll to being named employee of the month, you probably have accomplishments that are brag-worthy for scholarship applications.

On the other hand, if you don't have a lot of tangible honors and awards, don't be disheartened. There still may be time for you to earn some accolades. Look for competitions and events you can participate in that you might be particularly good at. In chapter 5, I discuss how to develop your credibility and track record for scholarship success.

ESSAYS

Applications typically list between one and five essay questions on a variety of topics. By asking students to share their thoughts, experiences, knowledge, and perspectives, essays give judges the opportunity to know the character and personality of an applicant. Much effort and forethought should be invested in developing engaging and compelling responses. In chapter 7, I discuss how to create winning essays that will stand out from the crowd and capture the judges' hearts.

LETTERS OF RECOMMENDATION

Letters of recommendation show scholarship judges that you are, in fact, just as fabulous as your application says you are! While scholarship committees may want to trust your word about yourself, they often choose to ask that you back up your claims with recommendations from people who know you well.

Teachers, coaches, and other credible sources can serve as star witnesses and write glowing recommendations that detail why you are the best candidate for a scholarship. In chapter 8, I discuss how to cultivate relationships with these people and ultimately receive stellar recommendation letters to support your scholarship application.

VARIABLES

The following items are required less often on scholarship applications; however, when they're requested, it means they are important.

Scholarship resumes are formal documents that list your activities and credentials and are required by many competitive scholarship programs. In chapter 8, I'll explain how to create a scholarship resume.

Interviews are necessary for some highly competitive programs, particularly for larger scholarships with the ability to fly in potential scholars from around the country. For example, when I completed the final round of the Coca-Cola Scholarship program, an interview was used to determine who ultimately won national awards. In chapter 9, I'll discuss interview techniques and preparation.

FAFSA results, as discussed in chapter 3, are used by need-based scholarships to determine if a student qualifies for assistance.

Auditions are often required by programs related to performance or the arts.

Sample work may be requested to demonstrate a specific skill or talent. For example, if you are applying to a scholarship program that targets aspiring journalists, a writing sample will likely be required.

You, Online

When you are considering dating someone or have just met a new friend, what's one of the first things you do? You check out his or her Facebook profile or Google the person's name to find out more about who the person is and his or her everyday life. Don't be fooled into thinking that scholarship and college admission committees don't do the same.

Though not often clearly stated in applications, a student's online presence is becoming an increasingly influential factor in scholar selection. According to Kaplan Test Prep's vice president of data science Jeff Olsen, "It's no longer uncommon for schools to check applicants' digital trails as part of the admissions evaluation. . . . Our overall message for all students: Since the Internet has a very long memory, use good judgment and be careful what you post."

You can tell the judges all about how wonderful you are in your application, but if they find drunken photos, profanity, and rude comments all over your Facebook wall, what are they going to believe? **Your attitude, your photos, the words you use, and the friends you associate with all constitute your online persona. Failing to care about the image you are portraying online can cost you dearly.**

Guarding Your Online Presence

Most students admit they have accepted a "friend request" from someone they have never met. If you post an inappropriate picture, anyone can simply download or take a screen shot of the image and post it online without permission. If a college or scholarship committee pulls up that image, they will most likely reconsider selecting you.

MAKING YOUR ONLINE PRESENCE WORK FOR YOU

The Internet can actually be a very important part of your college application process, helping you create a competitive advantage over other students. Scholarship officers want to know as much as they can about why you are the best choice for their award. Yet there are often limitations to what you can explain and how big of an impact you can have in a short application. With blogs, online magazines, YouTube, LinkedIn, and all the other tools available to you on the Internet, there are many ways you can make yourself even more appealing to the selection committees that look you up online!

Let's say you've made it to the semifinal round of a scholarship program. You are one of 25 applicants, but only 10 students will be selected as winners. All 25 of you are stellar applicants and you're all equally qualified, based on your applications. If the scholarship judges turn to the Internet as a tiebreaker, what will they find out about you that sets you apart from the other candidates? Will they find anything positive that helps support all the claims you've made in your application?

If you talk a lot in your application about a nonprofit that you started, for example, it would be nice if the first thing they see when they enter your name on Google is something like a news article about your work with the organization, a blog interview regarding a service event, and a link to a website you created for the organization. Also, a LinkedIn profile and personal website further highlighting your accomplishments can help elevate the judges' interest in you, distinguishing you from all other applicants. You can easily create a website using platforms like Weebly.com and Basekit.com.

Creating a significant online presence is less important than the officially judged areas of the application; still, don't let your online activity negatively reflect on you. Think strategically about your online presence, using the tools and resources available to make a positive impact on the people who can take your life to a new level. Such forethought will not only help you in the scholarship process but also as you seek college internships and move on into your chosen field after graduation.

SUMMARY POINTS

▶ *Scholarship varieties.* Thousands of scholarships are given out every year for all sorts of reasons. Dig around to find the ones that are the best fit for you and that set you up with the greatest chance of winning!

▶ *Need-based scholarships* factor a family's income into determining eligibility while *merit-based scholarships* focus on a student's personal qualities, actions, and achievements.

▶ The best *scholarship tools* to use for finding scholarships are scholarship reference books, online scholarship databases, your school's resources such as your guidance counselor, community-based scholarships, and looking into what scholarships are available at the schools you hope to attend.

▶ *Scholarship applications* are composed of grades, test scores, extracurricular activities, honors and awards, essays, and letters of recommendation. Some scholarships also evaluate applicants by using resumes, interviews, financial need, auditions, sample work, and your online presence.

ACTION STEPS

○ Make a list of at least 15 scholarships you want to apply to in the next 12 months. Put them in an ordered list, sorted by deadlines. Post the list somewhere visible and update it as you decide on any additional scholarships to apply to.

○ Create a list of all of the extracurricular activities you have participated in while in high school as well as the honors and awards you have earned.

○ Do an evaluation of your online persona and rate yourself on a scale of 1-10. Come up with a list of five ideas you can implement to improve your online image.

5

STANDING OUT

Creating Your Own Formula for Success

It's not uncommon for scholarship selection committees to review *thousands* of applications each year. Among them they see countless perfect GPAs, numerous student government leaders, and a multitude of sports stars. So when yours is the 10,000th application they evaluate, how are you going to make sure you're remembered?

One of the things I found most surprising in attending scholarship awards ceremonies and scholar conferences was the diversity of the winners' backgrounds and experiences. While I did meet winners with perfect grades and test scores, it was really great to meet so many students out there like me! Students who didn't have perfect scores or backgrounds but who worked really hard anyway and achieved scholarship success.

While a solid academic background is important—and something you should strive for—most scholarship programs aren't *just* looking for the smartest kids or the ones who win everything. Their priority is to find students with the potential and desire to make a significant contribution to the world.

You may be thinking, *Well, how can I prove I have that?*

The good news is, there are lots of ways!

In this chapter, I'll discuss key factors that can take you and your application from being just another one in the crowd to one that WOWS the committee into remembering you!

Sell Yourself!

My mom always said, "Sell yourself!" when I was filling out my scholarship applications. I didn't really understand what she meant until I got knee-deep in the process. If you are humble or shy by nature, you are probably inclined to downplay your accomplishments and make them seem more commonplace. Well, if ever there is a time to brag, your scholarship application is it! My mom used to always encourage me to act like a salesperson when filling out scholarship applications. I thought it was strange at first, but in hindsight, it's genius!

During his rise to fame, country artist Garth Brooks took an interesting approach to "selling" himself that we all can learn from: he learned to separate himself as a person from his business persona—a trick he learned in college while earning a degree in marketing. When discussing the business side of his music career, Garth would always refer to himself in third person. In other words, he could step back and look at the entertainer part of himself as a product to sell, strategically thinking through how "Garth Brooks" could impact his "customers," the fans.

Why don't you try it? Go ahead and put on your best salesperson's hat when filling out your scholarship applications. **Think of yourself as a product that you have to convince investors to invest their money in. Are you worth investing a $20,000 scholarship in? Of course you are! So sell them on it!** By the time you submit your application, you want it to be compelling enough that the judges know their search is over and they should invest their thousands of dollars in you.

To sell yourself, you need to know what "the investor" is looking for.

Getting to Know a Scholarship Program

Make sure you understand these two things about any scholarship program before you apply:

1. The *Why*. Each scholarship program has its own reasons for giving out award money—whether it's wanting to help produce future leaders, motivating volunteers who will go on to impact the world, or supporting people who make a prom dress from duct tape (yes, there is a scholarship for that). As much as possible, you need to learn what is motivating the organization's generosity before filling out an application.

2. The *Who*. Each scholarship organization also has its own definition of an ideal candidate. By unearthing the scholarship program's reasons and motivation for giving away money, you can get a better idea of what the organization is looking for in a scholarship winner.

RESEARCH

How do you go about getting that information? Survey the organization's website, brochure, database descriptions, and any other useful information you can find. If you are still unable to get a clear picture, don't hesitate to call the organization's office and ask for more insight. All the data you gather will help you gain a clearer picture of what the program is looking for.

Take note of areas the organization stresses and how things are stated:

- What descriptive words are used to describe candidates and values? (For example, you might see such words as *overcome, perseverance, ambition.*)
- Are certain themes or words repeatedly mentioned?
- Does the organization place a high value on community service? If so, is one certain area of community service mentioned more than others?
- What similarities do previous winners of this scholarship share?

OUTLINE

From this research, using the hints you've gathered and the qualities the scholarship program seems to value most, you can then develop an outline of that organization's ideal candidate. Break down your outline even further by including ways you fit the picture of that ideal candidate.

This outline can help you customize your application to specifically appeal to the scholarship program you are applying to. Reference it as you're filling out the scholarship application, thinking through how you embody the characteristics of the program's ideal candidate. For example, if you were applying to the Best Buy Scholarship program, your outline would include the fact that they value community service and, obviously, technology. When filling out this application, you'd want to spend extra time highlighting your volunteer experience. And any volunteer experience related to technological advancement would be toward the top of your list. If the essay topic is, "Discuss a moment in your life that made a significant impact," then highlighting a situation where you introduced technology to assist people in need with a charity you are passionate about would be a smart approach.

Outlines are quick, simple tools that help you craft responses in a way that lets judges know you took the time to get to know their program, you're a great candidate for their award—and you really want their scholarship.

. . . .

Check out TheCollegeNinja.com for a sample outline and other resources.

. . . .

Be Prepared—and Pleasant

When you call a scholarship organization, start by asking who you can speak with for more information, and make sure you have specific questions prepared. The people taking your calls are usually happy to answer any questions about the application process. Remember to treat anyone you speak with as if he or she is a scholarship judge—because that just might be the case! Some major scholarship programs keep records of all correspondence with potential scholars—including phone conversations. Don't underestimate the power your communication with these individuals can have. Even if a scholarship organization does not keep detailed phone records, many of them are small enough that word can easily get around about any not-so-positive correspondence or communication. Just be polite, friendly, and organized in your conversations, and you'll have nothing to worry about.

Academic Achievement

The truth is, when it comes to scholarships, you can have less-than-perfect grades, as I did, but those imperfect grades mean you will have to work harder in other areas to make up the difference. When you're up against students with better grades or higher test scores, and academics are a factor in the judging, you can't expect to win the scholarships if you're doing nothing more than they do. I will show you how to shine even if you struggle academically. However, you need to be willing to work for it!

That being said, it's no secret that academic achievement is often highly valued in the scholarship process. In fact, some scholarships are based solely on academic achievement. While some programs do not request or judge schoolwork, being prepared in this way opens the door to a much broader range of scholarships.

Academic achievement is not just limited to the confines of a classroom. It can be demonstrated through participation in learning-related organizations and activities such as the Foreign Language Club or Quiz Bowl Team. Independent research projects such as those you'd complete for a science competition can qualify as well.

It is also important to note that scholarship judges often pay attention to *trends* in your grades. If you didn't have the best grades as a freshman but you continually improve throughout high school, you demonstrate that you have learned from your experience. The sooner you realize this and start working to have a strong academic record, the better prepared you will be in both your scholarship and college applications.

Here are some tips about core areas judges use for academic evaluation: coursework, GPA, class rank, and standardized test scores.

COURSEWORK

The level of difficulty in your classes is important. Advanced Placement (AP), honors, and college-credit courses demonstrate that you are willing to challenge yourself but also that you are likely to be ready for the rigors of college. Don't wait until your senior year to try to squeeze in a bunch of hard classes. The earlier you start challenging yourself, the easier it will be to achieve a solid academic record.

GRADE POINT AVERAGE

The GPA requirement is different for each scholarship program, so familiarize yourself with the programs you plan on applying to. Some scholarships will ask students to verify their GPA with an official transcript. Contact your high school's administrative office to learn its transcript-request process so you're ready to supply what's needed.

CLASS RANK

This is a measure of how well your grades compare to those of the rest of the students in your class. Some scholarships use this as a way to evaluate applicants. Many schools have a formal system for determining your rank. If you are unsure what your class rank is—or *if* your school ranks—ask your guidance counselor.

STANDARDIZED TEST SCORES

Certain scholarship programs require you to share your standardized test scores (PSAT, SAT, or ACT). Even if the scholarship programs you want to apply to don't require test scores, it is wise to prepare carefully for standardized tests since they are a factor in most college applications. Make use of the numerous books, apps, and online resources available to help you prepare for these tests.

Certain scholarship programs simply trust you to share your test scores on the application while others require you to have the test's administrators submit your scores. Refer to the ACT and SAT official websites for more information about registering for those tests, what to have on the day of the test and how to get your scores sent to the right place. And for advice on preparing for standardized tests, please see the Q&A from Dr. Jay Rosner, admissions test expert and executive director of the Princeton Review Foundation, in the Resources section at the back of this book.

Extracurricular Activities

Extracurricular activities fall outside of normal schoolwork and include everything from sports to clubs to volunteer work to employment to church involvement. Scholarship programs often evaluate students' extracurricular involvement and achievement starting with their freshman year of high school.

With proper planning, a little strategy, and simply doing the things you love, you can really stand out in this area of the application.

RANGE VERSUS INTENSITY

Every student applying for scholarships is involved in his or her own unique combination of extracurricular activities. This personal combination of activities varies in what I like to call *range* and *intensity*. I use the word *range* to describe the amount and variety of activities a student has participated in. Intensity, on the other hand, is how heavily involved and accomplished the applicant is within his or her activities. Range demonstrates well-roundedness and the ability to balance multiple areas of life whereas intensity demonstrates your time commitment and achievement. **Having a strong blend of both range and intensity is ideal in scholarship applications.**

To restate it simply:

- Range = the amount and variety of your activities
- Intensity = your level of involvement and what you accomplished

BROADENING YOUR RANGE

Developing range mostly involves your ability to commit to activities. Fortunately, this can be fun and easy!

The most important thing in this area is to find activities you enjoy. For some students, this comes very naturally. But if you begin the scholarship process and realize you need more range, the sooner you begin working toward that goal, the better.

In other words, think about the things you love and how you could become part of a group of people who share your interests. Even if the only hobby you really enjoy is playing video games, then build a gaming network with a community of followers and develop a blog in which you share your tips and tricks online. You might even look into starting a video game club at school.

Yes, it's really that simple. A lot of people think that having range takes a ton of time. Not necessarily. There are plenty of activities you can participate in that don't require a huge time commitment. Especially if you join clubs or groups that meet during school hours or immediately before or after school. While I was in high school, I added several activities to my resume that didn't take much time outside of regular school hours, such as Fellowship of Christian Athletes, Varsity Women's Club, peer tutoring, Business Professionals of America, and show choir.

If you are panicking a little right now . . . take a deep breath and then get to work! It is rarely ever too late to broaden your range. Just keep this in mind: simply setting out to develop range by participating in activities that "look good" to judges doesn't work well. **Get involved in a variety of things that are fun for you—and your range will take care of itself!**

DEEPENING YOUR INTENSITY

Intensity is a bit harder to develop than range. It takes a deeper commitment to activities and is usually something that builds over time.

Awards, honors, and the investment of time that comes with long-term involvement are things that reflect intensity. Years of dedication to a few things you really excel in can be more appealing in scholarship applications than participating in a ton of activities that require little commitment.

If you are already a senior, reflect on the activities you have devoted the most time and energy to, and what are you most proud of. Make sure these activities are reflected in your application. If you are younger, start planning early and work hard: when you find activities you are really passionate about, pour yourself into them and give your best effort. Find ways you can go above and beyond just being involved in the activities; for example, consider taking on leadership roles, entering competitions, or completing specialized training. In doing this, you will naturally develop the intensity that stands out in scholarship applications—and you are more likely to excel as well.

Don't forget the nontraditional activities you've been involved in either. Working the same after-school job throughout high school can show intensity, as can taking care of your baby sister every day. Just be clear on how the depth of your experiences has positively influenced you to become the fantastic person you are today.

CREATING OPPORTUNITIES

Some of my favorite memories in high school, and some of the extracurricular activities that made me stand out the most in my scholarship applications, came from opportunities I created for myself. For example, during my sophomore year of high school I put together a shoe drive for Haiti and Tanzania—two countries where many people die each year because parasites enter their bodies through their feet.

For this project, I spent a few hours making flyers and phone calls to get the word out, and then a few hours each week to keep things going. That minimal time commitment not only potentially saved several lives but it enriched mine as well. It also went a long way toward making me a more desirable scholarship candidate. Since nobody else had that activity on their application, it helped make mine unique and memorable.

You too should brainstorm creative things you can do. If you feel like you're struggling to think of something, sit down with family and friends and bounce ideas off of each other. Here is a four-step process for creating your own opportunities:

Evaluate Available Time. How many hours a week or month do you have to commit to a new venture? How long do you *want* to devote to it (a week, a few months, years)?

Evaluate Interests. What are you passionate about? What are you good at?

Get Creative! Brainstorm ideas that are realistically within your time constraints *and* that match your interests. If you look long enough and think outside the box, you will find something you love doing, which makes it way more worthwhile.

Evaluate Resources. What resources are at your disposal to help you with your new venture? Who do you know that can help? Does it cost money? Lots of time? Require a lot of people? Make sure the opportunity you create fits the resources you have access to.

As you set out on your quest to get involved in extracurricular activities, keep track of each involvement for easier recall when filling out scholarship applications. Also, keep records of any honors, awards, and accolades you receive. Judges like to see the results of your efforts.

Your activities can go a long way in helping you stand out in your scholarship applications. They can also be some of the greatest highlights of your high school experience. Now get out there and enjoy yourself!

Worry about Yourself

I was ranked number 32 out of 182 students in my senior class based on GPA. Twelve students in my class had flawless 4.0 GPAs, and I obviously wasn't one of them. Still, I was applying to national scholarship programs. How could I hope to win against thousands of applicants across the country when I wasn't even close to being one of the top students in my own small-town school?

My classmates would often talk about who they thought was going to win XYZ hometown scholarship for $500, and I wasn't even on their radar. If no one thought I could ever win the favored local scholarships, then did I really have a chance to win the huge nationwide scholarships I was trying for? Was I wasting my time?

These are the kinds of thoughts that would occasionally run through my mind. Fortunately, from a very young age, I was taught by my mom to think outside the box. She wanted me to realize there is a great big world beyond the limitations of where I was born and the situation I was in.

So many of my peers were focused on who they assumed would win the few local scholarships that they failed to even begin looking outside our community. Ironically, though I was number 32 in my class of 182 students, I was one of 50 students from across the country chosen as a Coca-Cola National Scholar out of more than 100,000 applicants! I was also selected from more than 60,000 students to be a Gates Scholar.

As it turned out, not one of the students in my class won more scholarship money than I did, even though I often felt like the underdog. If I had allowed myself to worry about the 31 classmates ahead of me, I never would have won *any* scholarships. So don't allow yourself to be intimidated by your peers or your circumstances. They have no part in determining your capabilities or your scholarship potential. Only you can do that.

Yes, it can be discouraging to hear your classmates talk about how well they did on their SATs and how great their GPAs are, especially if your scores aren't as high. But take it from someone who had average test scores and less-than-perfect grades: *don't let this distract you from your goal!* Even if there are stellar students ahead of you who will win big scholarships, the only way they can take away your potential is if you let them intimidate you into not even trying.

Think of it this way instead: developing your application is like a competition against yourself. Do the absolute best *you* can do to prepare to win scholarships, recognizing that scholarship judges look for a variety of factors in winners and that no two scholars are exactly the same. **Rather than worrying about other students who are applying for scholarships, put that extra effort into learning how to best prepare yourself for success.**

Don't let the fear of competition keep you from applying for scholarships. It's okay to know what kind of competition you're up against, but let that competition motivate you rather than worry you. Being a little anxious about the scholarship process is normal. You must press through the anxiety anyway and find the confidence to give it your best shot.

I encourage you to step outside the box—and expect to be surprised and delighted with the results.

SUMMARY POINTS

▶ *Get to know the scholarship programs* you are applying to. Find out what they are all about and their purpose for giving out scholarships. Create an outline for each scholarship to help you customize your applications to that program.

> Scholarship applicants should strive to have a balance between the *range* and *intensity* of activities they participate in. *Range* refers to the amount of activities a student participates in whereas *intensity* refers to the time and commitment a student has made in those activities.

> *Creating your own opportunities* can be easier than you think, and it will go a long way on scholarship applications. If you haven't found structured activities you enjoy and/or you like to be creative, you can blaze your own path!

> Don't let *the competition* intimidate you. Scholarship programs aren't just looking for students with perfect academic backgrounds. I'm proof that you don't have to be the "picture perfect" student to win a lot of scholarships!

ACTION STEPS

O Using the list of 15 or more scholarships that you developed in the previous chapter's action steps, get to know each scholarship program. Create an outline to use for each of the scholarships you plan on applying for.

O Using the four steps for *creating opportunities*, come up with three unique activities you could implement within the next year.

6

SCHOLAR QUALITIES

The Makings of a Winner

I've had the pleasure of meeting and interviewing several major scholarship recipients from all types of backgrounds. They've ranged from average students to valedictorians and computer whizzes to star athletes.

While many of them seemed to have nothing in common, judging by first appearance, as I spoke with each one of them, I discovered what tied them all together: each one possessed certain "scholar qualities" that positively influenced how they approached life, their passions, and their futures.

Though first impressions might lead someone to think that many of them were ordinary teens, these qualities helped make them extraordinary and let them stand out from other students.

These certain qualities—character, leadership, teamwork, volunteerism, work ethic, purpose, and initiative—are what almost every scholarship program seeks in its winners. When evaluating applications, scholarship judges "read between the lines" to see if an applicant demonstrates these qualities. They use your list of activities and achievements, answers to essay questions, recommendation letters, and other variables discussed throughout this book to determine if you are "it."

Be sure to keep these scholar qualities in mind as you're filling out your application—and find ways to express them if they describe you. Otherwise, the scholarship judges may not realize you have what they are looking for.

That being said, it's not about trying to be someone you're not. **Knowing the scholar qualities helps you better reflect who you are and learn to accentuate the admirable qualities that make you great.**

CHARACTER

How do you behave when no one is watching? Do you continue to uphold your values even when you face opposition? *Character* has been defined as "moral or ethical strength." With the goal of selecting future leaders and world changers, scholarship organizations hope for scholars who possess great character.

Scholarship essays are one important way you can demonstrate character. For example, you could display character when discussing how you handled a difficult situation or overcame an obstacle.

Stay true to who you are and what you believe, and character will be a natural result.

LEADERSHIP

Do you step up when direction is needed? Do you inspire others to follow you? While participating in a variety of extracurricular activities is good, scholarship programs like to see students step up and take on leadership roles in the things they love best. For example, becoming captain of the swim team, organizing a club fund-raiser every year, or coaching in a youth soccer league are all ways to display leadership abilities. You're never too young to be a leader and make a significant impact in your school, your community, and the world.

TEAMWORK

Do you work well with others? Are you able to be productive as a member of a group? Teamwork means you partner effectively with others and make meaningful contributions in a group setting, even when you're not in charge. Participating in team sports, group projects, or academic clubs where each person's effort contributes to a collective result can be used to demonstrate teamwork on a scholarship application. Being able to positively fulfill your role as part of a team is a very important skill, not only for scholarship applications but in life itself.

VOLUNTEERISM

Commitment to others and to causes beyond yourself is a very important quality to most scholarship panels. Remember that in a judge's mind, scholarships are given as an act of service in an effort to make someone's life better. So scholarship committees place a high value on students who are serving their community—even the world—in creative and compelling ways, expecting them to continue to give of themselves and essentially pay it forward as they find success.

The Power of Volunteering

Don't ever underestimate the power of volunteer work. It not only can enrich your scholarship application but it can transform your life!

Volunteering is an opportunity to help other people while also helping yourself. When you volunteer and become involved in community service, you learn a lot about yourself and others, which causes you to grow and become a better person. While you are becoming a better person, you are also becoming a better scholarship applicant. Judges love to see applicants who have readily given their time and energy to help other people.

Even though my family didn't have a lot to give in material wealth, I knew there were still people who could use my help. So by the time I graduated from high school, I had logged more than 1,000 community service hours.

The time I spent investing in my community and volunteering in high school also seemed to open up the floodgates of blessing in my own life, allowing me to win more money in scholarships than I ever could have earned in 1,000 hours of minimum-wage work. I strongly believe that giving back and helping others in their time of need opens the door for God to bless us big time.

It is easy to become a volunteer leader and start your own projects as well. Doing so gives you a way to demonstrate your leadership skills on applications. As you volunteer, keep a record of the activities you participate in and your hours so you can accurately recall the details when filling out scholarship applications.

WORK ETHIC

Though college can be a ton of fun, there's hard work involved too. At Vanderbilt, the common saying was "Work Hard, Play Hard." The key to that slogan is *work*.

How well do you work? And how hard? Do you put your entire self into what you do?

Find what you love and give it your best. When you're doing what you love and working because you want to, it's easy to authentically demonstrate a good work ethic. At 16, I took that "find what you love and give it your best" approach when I went looking for a job at the gymnastics facility where I used to train. When I got there, I found out my old team no longer existed. What did I do about it? I started a new one! In spite of initially having only three girls on the team, I kept at it every week until the group grew to 40 girls. I spent at least 12 hours a week at the gym, coordinating competitions, training staff, and coaching my girls; I also spent countless unpaid hours planning at home.

I was doing something I loved and having fun. I didn't realize at the time that I was also demonstrating a strong work ethic. But I eventually used this experience to illustrate work ethic in my scholarship applications.

Three areas of your work ethic are most relevant to scholarship judges: effort, responsibility, and perseverance. Let's look at each one of those areas.

Effort. Are you willing to put forth the time and energy needed to get the job done? Will you push yourself to perform at a high level even when you don't feel like it?

History is filled with people who became successful primarily because they motivated themselves to work harder than everyone else. Effort can help you overcome most of the challenges you will ever face in college or your career, making it an important quality in scholars.

Responsibility. Do you take personal *responsibility* for your actions? Are you accountable for the choices you make? When someone trusts you with a task, how do you handle it? In college, you don't have your parents or a boss always checking up on you and making sure you're doing what you're supposed to; therefore, being accountable for your own actions is very important.

College offers a lot of freedom, and it's up to you to get things done when they need to be. Some students don't bear that responsibility well and ultimately don't make it through. Scholarship committees want to know that you are mature enough to handle the freedom of college and that you will make the most of their investment in you.

Perseverance. Do you continue to put forth effort despite challenges, opposition, or failure? When things get tough, do you get even more determined, or do you give up? It's okay to admit on your application that you have failed or endured hardships, but be aware that seeing how you forged ahead and overcame the obstacles is important to scholarship judges.

PURPOSE

Why do you do what you do? Are your actions rooted in a sense of *purpose*—a reason beyond yourself? Planning to study medicine in college with the goal of working in an area of cancer research that claimed the life of a loved one would exemplify moving forward with a sense of purpose. Purpose is not only an important quality for scholars, but it also can carry someone through good times and bad.

For example, I'm moving with purpose in writing this book. After really struggling through much of my life, I found my way out of my hardships and on to success.

This book is enabling me to help students in similar circumstances navigate their way to success more quickly and easily than I was able to.

In each thing you get involved in, look beyond *what* you're doing and discover *why* you're doing it.

INITIATIVE

When there is something you really want, do you go for it? Do you go out of your way to make positive change that didn't exist before you got involved? To put it simply, *initiative* is taking action when no one is pushing you to.

Most scholarship programs love it when students don't just wait for change to happen but go out and make it happen themselves. Hosting a fundraiser for a charity you are passionate about, raising money to go on a missions trip, or planning study sessions for your classmates are all indicators of initiative. This quality in a scholarship applicant shows that you have the tools and desire to lead positive change.

Quality Advertising!

Knowing the qualities you want to "advertise" on an application is one thing, but how can you actually demonstrate those qualities for the scholarship judges? The best place is often within your essays. They're one of the most important parts of the scholarship application, because they give you the opportunity to strategically share more information about yourself. Consider them your own 30-second commercial, promoting yourself.

We will talk more about crafting essays later in the book, but for now, I'd like to show you one of my essays that helped me win several scholarships. Read it with the goal of identifying how the various scholar qualities can be demonstrated in only a few paragraphs. I've used all caps and boxes below to make it easy for you to find the parts of the essays pertaining to the scholar qualities.

Question: Write about the community service activity that is most meaningful to you (in fewer than 225 words).

Answer: The experiences that have impacted me the most are *mission trips* VOLUNTEERISM. Since my first trip to Haiti, I have seen the world from a different perspective. *It made me realize what I have and not to take it for granted* CHARACTER. Not only did this trip open my eyes to the many contributions I can give and things I can do, *it also inspired me to take a stand for those who cannot stand for themselves* LEADERSHIP.

Thousands of people die every year from parasites entering their bodies through their feet. We live in a very fortunate country, where many people discard several pairs of shoes each year. Each pair of unwanted shoes could be a life saved. *I have developed a project* INITIATIVE to assist in preventing this unfortunate form of death. *Working with my community* TEAMWORK, *I have sent hundreds of shoes* WORK ETHIC to Haiti, Liberia, and Tanzania, hopefully saving hundreds of lives.

In Haiti, it was not uncommon to see a person lying in the road on the verge of death or having an open wound with no one to help. *A long-term goal* PURPOSE I am passionate about is to one day be able to provide funding and assistance to build a fully staffed, nonprofit medical center in the poverty stricken town of Jeremy. With hard work and perseverance, anything is attainable.

Your Personal Touch

While the scholar qualities discussed in this chapter give you an idea of what scholarship programs are looking for, every person demonstrates them differently. Now it's time to take these characteristics and give them your own twist by embracing your uniqueness, highlighting your strengths, and strengthening your weaknesses.

EMBRACING YOUR UNIQUENESS

We all have qualities that make us who we are and separate us from everyone else. Some of us try to hide our uniqueness until we finally wake up one day and realize that being unique is cool!

Without your uniqueness, you could easily blend into the crowd, which is not what you want to do in a scholarship application! So let go of any stereotypes regarding the "ideal scholarship candidate" and accept that you are one of a kind. Then celebrate it! Use your uniqueness to find the activities you are good at and to create opportunities other people haven't thought of.

As you look for those opportunities, make sure you are molding them around who *you* really are. You'll do much better if you're excelling in things you love versus just trying to become someone you think scholarship committees want.

Learn to embrace your positive, unique qualities, and then demonstrate how they make you a great choice for a scholarship!

Common sense tells you that spotlighting your strengths in a scholarship application is important. But it is also important to highlight the strengths that make you *different*.

If you feel that your strengths are pretty common, brainstorm how you can build on them so that you positively stand out from other applicants with similar interests. For example, I really enjoy music and spent a lot of time working on it in high school, like a lot of kids do. On my application, I emphasized how I sang in the high school choir, but I also shared that I had made it a priority to share my talents by setting up shows at nursing homes, hospitals, and charity events.

We are all good at *something*, though *your* something may be nontraditional. When it comes to scholarships, though, nontraditional can be a plus. Lots of class presidents, valedictorians, and high school football stars will be applying for scholarships. Yet those wonderful accomplishments can sometimes get lost in the shuffle of a highly competitive applicant pool if they are not highlighted effectively. Those high achievers can get beat out by applicants with less glamorous accomplishments simply because those applicants were better able to articulate their strengths and separate themselves from the crowd.

How do you highlight your strengths? Create "hooks" in your application that will catch a scholarship judge's attention. Share what you have done to go above and beyond your peers who have a similar title, interest, or achievement. For example, the sport I was most active in when I was younger was gymnastics. Plenty of high schoolers do gymnastics, but I created a distinction by going beyond that to become a coach and start my own team.

If you are a class president, what have you done in your role to make a significant impact in your school that other class presidents throughout the country haven't done? If you are a track athlete who hasn't won many awards, how can you demonstrate a superior level of commitment and leadership within the sport?

We all have the potential to show great strength in something. Reflect on the activities you love and are good at. Write down the characteristics that make you unique. Brainstorm ways you can build on those strong areas and demonstrate your "scholar qualities" within them. When you've done that, articulating your strengths becomes a whole lot easier.

STRENGTHEN YOUR WEAKNESSES

Just as we all have our own strengths, we also have our weaknesses. So we must learn to fill in the gaps on our applications that reveal those weaknesses.

In the scholarship process, your weaknesses are those areas where you lack the ability to fully demonstrate academic achievement, extracurricular activities, or a specific scholar quality. Perhaps you are strong academically but have few extracurricular activities. Or maybe you have a long list of extracurricular activities but little of it is volunteer work. Or maybe you've worked often in a group setting but without taking any leadership roles. While your strengths are important and should be highlighted, taking the time to strengthen your weaknesses will make you a more well-rounded scholarship applicant.

So how do you do this? The earlier you start planning for scholarship applications, the simpler it is. Here are a few key steps:

1. Print off applications for scholarships you know you want to apply for or look at the application worksheet in the Resource section at the end of this book.

2. Work through the different application elements and essay questions to define areas where you are lacking (such as volunteer work, initiative, extracurricular activities).

3. Evaluate what you are lacking in range or intensity in each category, and think through how you can take steps to improve each area. Which organizations, sports, and activities can you become involved in to fill in the gaps? **Stretching outside your comfort zone can actually be fun, as well as a good exercise to prepare you for the challenges of college.**

Filling the Gaps

If you are an underclassman and have time to participate in more activities and gain credentials, get busy! Quality involvement is always best. If you are closer to graduation but still need a few more items on your list, try to find what I call "gap fillers"—activities that take very little time but look great on a resume.

Most of the gap fillers I participated in were during school hours or for just less than an hour, and they only met occasionally. Likewise, you can look for things to do during school hours that only require a small time commitment, such as joining clubs that meet once a month for an hour or two. Many scholarships don't ask for the specific amount of time you've committed to each activity anyway.

That being said, gap fillers are only that: fillers. I don't recommend you go out and sign up for a bunch of random clubs you don't care about just so you can enhance your resume. You want to avoid laundry lists of activities without much quality involvement. Always strive first and foremost to find meaningful participation in activities whenever you can, while seeking to be well rounded.

If scholarship application deadlines are approaching and you're really struggling to come up with ways to compensate for your weaknesses, take time to reflect on the past and jot down the things you may have missed. For example, if you are lacking in community service hours, brainstorm situations where you went outside the norm to help other people. If you brought your neighbors together to clean up after a storm one year, you could list something like "Neighborhood Coordinator for Storm Cleanup." Though not an "official" volunteer activity, it *is* service, and it often counts!

I encourage you to be creative with how you strengthen your weaknesses and build on your strengths. **Remember what you learned in chapter 5. If it is late in the scholarship game and you have gaps that need to be filled, you can always think like an entrepreneur and create your own opportunities!** Use your new knowledge and wisdom to start filling in your gaps and build a rock-star application!

Succeeding after Failure

Many students worry about putting themselves out there and failing. It can feel risky to try things, knowing you may not be successful. However, your failures and bad experiences don't define your potential.

Sometimes standing out is just standing back up and trying again. Famous people throughout history struggled significantly in the areas they ultimately became most successful in. It's said that:

- *Walt Disney* tried becoming a newspaper cartoonist but was rejected by the industry and told by an editor that he "lacked imagination and had no good ideas."
- *Thomas Edison* was told by his teachers that he was "too stupid to learn anything."
- *Michael Jordan* was cut from his high school basketball team.
- *J. K. Rowling* was rejected by 12 publishers before a

small London-based publishing house agreed to sign her.

I've also experienced failures in the same areas I've experienced my greatest successes. I shared earlier about the incredible surprise of winning a pageant in which 191 other girls in my age group competed. That life-changing experience led me to believe maybe I could win another pageant if I tried.

I had watched the Miss Teen USA pageant on TV for years and dreamed about being on that stage. To get to the nationally televised pageant, contestants first had to win their state's Miss Teen USA pageant, which was notoriously competitive. So I decided to compete in a small, little-known pageant to test whether I had any chance at the state title.

It turned out there was only one other girl in my age group at this small pageant. Not only was it the other contestant's first time competing in a pageant, but she came down with pneumonia the evening before the competition and spent the night in the hospital. She showed up the next day feeling miserable, fumbled through her interview questions, and almost fell off the stage. Backstage, she talked about how awful she felt and how she couldn't wait to get the pageant over with. I thought surely I would win against a girl who was sick and didn't want to be there.

We stood on stage at the final awards ceremony, waiting for the winner's name to be called, and to our mutual surprise, runner-up went to . . . *me*! I had worked for weeks preparing for this tiny pageant, and I had put on my best show, only to lose to my lone competitor!

In that moment, I swore off pageants and told my mom I never wanted to do another one again. I then scooped up what was left of my pride and went home to pout. After a few days, though, my disappointment and frustration started shifting into thoughts about the Miss Teen USA pageant again. I still wrestled with self-doubt, but I finally decided I wasn't going to let one failure ruin my confidence or a chance to do something I really aspired to.

This time, I knew I was going to have to work even harder, so I spent months preparing for the Miss Indiana Teen USA pageant. I watched more than 50 hours of Teen USA pageant videos, and I analyzed everything previous winners had done to make them successful. I let friends and family members ask me the most intimidating and challenging interview questions to help me learn to think quickly. And I devoured any information I thought could help prepare me for success. This time, the hard work paid off, and I was crowned Miss Indiana Teen USA!

Because of my loss in the small pageant, I approached the Miss Indiana Teen USA event with a whole new sense of humility and focus that I never would have had if I hadn't been slapped with defeat. The memory of losing to the girl with pneumonia provided a constant reminder that I had to put forth my absolute best effort.

Losing a pageant with only two contestants was one of many moments of failure that later propelled me toward success. Throughout my life, people have called me lucky, but most of them never saw the number of times I was defeated and heartbroken. Every major win I celebrated usually came after several losses. What made me seem so "lucky" was that I just never gave up. Each time I lost, I took the time to learn what I could do better and then gave it another shot.

It's not if you fail or how often you fail that matters most but what you do *after* you fail. *That* is what determines how far you can go.

Learn to use failure to motivate and inspire yourself to work harder and more strategically the next time. I certainly know how frustrating failure or rejection can be in the moment, but it really does help victory taste that much sweeter when you reach it! As you prepare for scholarships and your future, become relentlessly determined to continue working hard toward your goals no matter the opposition that comes your way. The success you deserve is within your reach!

SUMMARY POINTS

▌ The most common *scholar qualities* used when evaluating scholarship applicants are character, leadership, teamwork, volunteerism, work ethic, purpose, and initiative.

▌ Your *uniqueness* helps you stand out from the rest of the scholarship applicants. Highlighting your strengths and strengthening your weaknesses helps you put your best foot forward when applying to scholarship programs.

▶ Countless scholars have *succeeded after failure*. Don't be afraid to put yourself out there and risk failing. Use any setbacks to motivate you toward success.

ACTION STEPS

○ Look at each *scholar quality* and write a short paragraph describing a situation in which you demonstrated that quality.

○ Fill out the first portion (up to the essay section) of the Scholarship Application Worksheet located in the Resources section of this book. It is modeled after real scholarship applications, requiring common criteria requested by most scholarships. Filling out the worksheet will help you identify your strengths, weaknesses, and areas for improvement. It will also help you start developing a blueprint for future applications.

TELLING YOUR STORY

Painting a Picture with Words

Filling out a scholarship application is all about telling a story—the story of who you are, where you've come from, and where you're going. It's important to tell the best, most compelling story possible in the limited space you have to show a scholarship committee why you are the best choice for their investment.

We all have a story—the journey that makes us who we are. As we navigate life's twists and turns on the way to our destiny, some of our roads are very winding and full of curves. Occasionally we hit dead ends, get flat tires, get lost, or crash. When facing those challenges, some people never get their car started again and live the rest of their lives stuck on the side of the road. Winners, on the other hand, restart their car and get moving again. What matters most is not that you never get lost or stuck . . . it's that you get back on the road and continue forward.

Sharing some parts of my story in scholarship applications

wasn't easy. I had to really push myself and dig deep to be able to open up to complete strangers about life experiences I hadn't shared with anyone else. When I sat down to write chapter 1 of this book, I again felt the uneasiness of sharing my personal story. Still, I pushed through the discomfort because there was a greater reward involved: I wanted everyone who reads this book—all who have ever encountered obstacles or felt they are not as smart or as good as everyone else—to know they can overcome and succeed!

The great thing about a personal story is that it has the power to evoke emotions in its readers and inspire them to action. That's as true for scholarship judges as anyone else. A lot of students are embarrassed to share the obstacles they've had to overcome to get to where they are. In fact, Vanessa Evans, associate director of the Ron Brown Scholarship, told me that one of the biggest mistakes students make on their applications is not telling their story. She explained, "We are trying to read between the lines to figure out who the person is. Students often tell us their GPA and class rank but forget to tell us *who they are*. We want to know how they became the person they are. We can get the academic achievement from the transcript, but we want to see what makes them tick."

When given the opportunity, many students only supply scholarship judges with a surface-level idea of who they are, leaving the committee nothing to remember but test scores and a list of activities. I encourage you to not only share the triumphs and achievements of your life but also the challenges you successfully overcame to get there. You have a unique story that carries the power to challenge, inspire, and motivate the people who read it. Learning to effectively share your story can have a tremendous impact on scholarship judges.

If you are still in the midst of some challenge and have not yet been able to find a positive outlook, I encourage you to keep pushing through, knowing there is hope. While life holds many things we can't control, it's important to work on the things we can. In the Resources section of this book, you can read "Scholar Stories" about other scholarship winners who endured significant challenges. The one thing these scholars have in common is that they took life one day at a time, focusing on the things they could control and working hard until they became successful. So hold your head up high, hold on to your faith, and keep pressing forward, knowing you're not alone and better days lie ahead.

In the scholarship process, essays give scholarship committees the chance to connect with you and see a picture of who you are as a person. This chapter discusses how to develop and present your story in a way that paints an unforgettable image of the incredible person you are and compels scholarship committees to believe in your potential for their program.

The Self-Portrait

Knowing who you are and being able to paint a clear, compelling picture of yourself is a critical part of earning scholarships. Think of each section of the application as a significant piece of the portrait.

You can draw a beautiful face, but if the hair is crazy or an eye is missing, it can drastically throw off the entire image and take away from the beauty in the rest of the portrait. So treat each section of the application with as much importance as the next. Determine what each section says about you and paint it well. This will help you develop a consistency in your story that allows each portion of the picture to fit together so that you come across as relatable and genuine.

Essays are essential to completing your portrait. Since you get to pick the direction of your response, they are more flexible than other areas of your application. This allows you to:

- direct your essays in a way that fill in missing parts of your portrait, or
- further explain parts you only briefly got to mention in another section.

I encourage you to take advantage of the opportunity essays provide to really evaluate what's needed to complete your portrait for the judges. When you're finished with your application, it will be a masterpiece you will be proud of for years to come!

Reflecting Your Best Self

In a scholarship application, you are drawing a picture of yourself with words. In order to draw the best, most accurate picture, you must look at your reflection. Reflect back on your life and think through the moments, the events, and the people who had the most impact on making you who you are. Who has had the greatest influence on you? What obstacles have you overcome, and what challenges have you prevailed against? What activities have been the most meaningful to you?

Schedule a date with yourself and sit down to really get to know *you*. It is much easier to draw a picture of something you already have a clear vision of rather than something stored vaguely in your memory.

Essay Effectiveness

Essays are one of the most important elements of the scholarship application. They give judges the opportunity to know your personality and distinguish you from the crowd. They also bring life to an application because they are personal. So while every area of the application is important, essays are where you really get to paint your picture and tell your story.

TOPICS

Essay topics can vary greatly between scholarships, although many scholarship programs follow similar themes. In general, scholarship essays fall into these main categories:

Past Experiences. Many scholarship essays are reflective and ask about life experiences you've had. They seek to understand how you perceived and handled certain situations.

Example: *Who has had the greatest influence on your life, and what did you learn from him or her?*

The Hypothetical. Some essays require you to give your perspective on how you would handle a given situation. When answering these questions, remember that the judges may not have the same opinion as you do. Express your opinion, but be careful not to alienate people who may not share your opinion or belief system. For example, avoid strong political statements or judgments.

Example: *If you were given $10,000 to aid a volunteer effort, how would you spend it?*

Perspective. Some scholarships ask questions that seek to understand your outlook on a variety of potential topics. They want to see how you respond to an idea or issue that requires your point of view.

Example: *How do you feel technology affects personal interaction among high school students?*

Knowledge-Based. This type of essay is about demonstrating your understanding of (and sometimes your perspective on) a given topic. Such questions are typically posed by programs that only accept applicants within a specific field of study, such as history or science.

Example: *Explain the importance of the battle of Gettysburg.*

Fun. Some scholarship programs have quirky, creative essay requirements such as asking you to come up with a recipe or share your zombie-apocalypse escape plan.

Example: *If you could be any type of candy, what would you be and why?*

FIRST STEPS

The hardest step in writing a scholarship essay is often the first step: beginning to write. If you're like me, you start out wanting the essay to be so perfect that you scare yourself out of starting at all.

I wish I could say there is a magic solution for getting the ball rolling, but unfortunately, there's not. However, thanks to the many essays I've written, I have developed a couple of *very* helpful tricks that I want to pass along to you.

Brainstorm bubbles are my best trick for writing essays, especially long ones. I sometimes struggle with knowing where to start and with organizing all my thoughts. Getting out a clean sheet of paper and breaking down my thoughts into what I call "brainstorm bubbles" helps me solidify my ideas so that writing the essay is easier. Here is an example of a brainstorm for one of my scholarship essays:

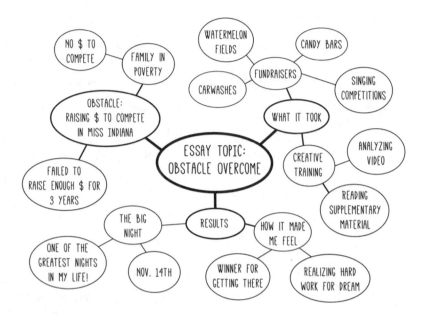

Example essay question: *Describe an obstacle you faced as a leader in an academic, extracurricular, or personal endeavor. How did you overcome barriers to success?*

1. Start off with the essay topic as the middle bubble. The main branches extending from that bubble are the key topics you want to cover in the essay.

2. From there, make smaller branches and bubbles that break down what you want to say within each area.

3. Once you have created your bubble-breakdown, you can develop a thorough outline for your essay.

4. Once you have an outline, the hardest part is over, and you can move forward with your writing.

(P.S. This trick has come in extremely handy in college too!)

Free Writing. If you sit down to write and find yourself staring at a blank page for more than five minutes, try free writing. Set a timer for 20 minutes, and just start typing or scribbling down whatever comes to mind about the topic at hand. Even if you throw out everything you write, this exercise will help you get your thoughts out of your head and into beginning the writing process. Most often, though, I am surprised at how useful the results are.

Sometimes I use these brainstorming tricks even when I know what I want to write about. Not only do they help me get my thoughts straight, but they also ensure that I don't miss out on an important selling point or a better angle to write from.

My Final Essay

At age seven, I lost my father to cancer. Since his death, my family has been classified as below poverty level. Regardless of our circumstances, my mother always told me I could achieve anything I set my mind to. I set a goal to one day be in the Miss Teen USA pageant.

For three years, I registered to compete in Miss Indiana Teen USA but couldn't continue because I fell drastically short of the $995 entry fee. I was determined this past year to find a way to be on stage in November and have a shot at my dreams.

I worked night and day to raise the money and prepare for the pageant. I worked in the watermelon fields, coordinated numerous car washes, sold candy bars every day, and participated in singing competitions. I could not afford training, so I spent many hours reading supplementary materials and watching videos.

I went into the pageant already feeling like a winner, just for making it that far. On the night of November 14, my dreams came true as I was crowned the winner! I will now move on to the Miss Teen USA pageant on national television! In light of my success, I will never forget my roots and what it took to achieve my dream.

Essay Tips

Put yourself in the position of a scholarship judge. You have to read 200 different essays on the same topic from numerous students in the course of a day or two, and then narrow down those 200 applicants to the 10 you like most. How would you do it?

You'd pick the ones you remember most.

From my conversations with scholarship program personnel and college admissions officials, that approach is actually very representative of the scholarship selection process. Making an impression that judges remember is important in your essays. The following tips will help your essays stand out:

MAKE EACH WORD COUNT

Scholarship judges have to read through hundreds of applications to find their winners, which means you must capture and keep their attention with every word you write. A lot of scholarship essays also have word limits of 250 or fewer, which means you absolutely have to make every word count.

The first draft of your essay does not need to be perfect. Write what you need to without much concern for word limits; then start chiseling it down by evaluating every sentence and every word. Ask yourself, *How can I say this in a more precise, effective way? Is this word or phrase really necessary to get my point across?* Repeat this process until your essay not only fits within the allowed word count but also uses only targeted words that take your essay a step deeper.

Think about this process like your Twitter or Facebook status updates. Some people choose to use the limited space they are given to write meaningless or mindless mini-reports while others make the most of the 140 characters they're given. You've seen the updates that are incredibly moving, telling a story in just a short amount of space and garnering a huge response from friends.

Twitter and Facebook can be incredible mechanisms that teach you how to write compellingly in short spaces. **When writing essays, think through how each word will touch everyone reading it and move the judges to respond positively.**

SHOW, DON'T TELL

In your essays, don't just *tell* the judges how awesome you are. *Prove it!* Show them through stories and specific examples that you exemplify the admirable qualities they're looking for.

Let's say, for example, you are applying for a scholarship that values volunteerism. You want to communicate that you are very service-oriented. In this situation, many students simply repeat what judges could already gather from the list of activities in their application. A more effective approach is to share a story about a specific time when you proved you had what the scholarship organization is looking for. Don't just say you have a passion for volunteerism; instead, share how your passion has caused you to take steps to make a difference and what the impact has been.

Like they always say, actions speak louder than words—and that couldn't be truer when filling out a scholarship application.

Don't Be Redundant!

Hall of Fame songwriter and record producer Fred Foster once told me, "It's okay to be repetitive when writing a song. Just don't be redundant!" I believe that's also true for scholarship applications. Don't make the mistake of making your essays boring resumes full of facts you've already shared in your application. Use your essays to go further in letting the judges know what makes you special and why you are different from all their other applicants.

KEEP IT PERSONAL

In the short space you have in your essays and application, you want to make the judges feel like they already know you and have a personal connection with you. The best way to do that is by getting personal when the opportunity presents itself.

It may feel uncomfortable to share your stories and triumphs with someone you've never met, but it actually helps you stand out from the crowd in the judges' minds. In several of my scholarship essays, I shared stories of obstacles I'd overcome that I hadn't even shared with some of my best friends. Not every scholarship essay will require you to get personal, but the impact can usually be so much greater if you do.

What If There's No Drama?

In case you're worried that you don't have a dramatic enough "picture to paint," I want to say . . . DON'T WORRY. You don't have to have faced obstacles to be a great scholarship candidate. There are many ways to demonstrate your scholar qualities in essays.

Don't disqualify yourself if you can't immediately think of anything engaging or significant in your life story. Sometimes it just takes a little more reflection and digging deeper. You may not be seeing something you've experienced as significant, when someone else would. For example, I was recently talking with a close friend who went to college on a full academic scholarship. After hearing me speak on scholarships, he expressed how thankful he was that he had gotten an academic-based scholarship from a small private college, because he didn't feel like he had much of a life story to tell for essays: his parents were still alive and married to each other, he didn't have any health issues, and he had enjoyed a very happy childhood overall.

I started reflecting on what I knew of his childhood based on what he'd told me in past conversations, and I was able to paint the picture of his life story in a compelling way he had never thought of. I told him, "If I were painting the picture of your story, I'd say . . ."

Justin grew up in the middle of the woods in Arkansas. His family didn't have heating or air conditioning; they got their water from the creek that ran through their yard; and they didn't even have their own phone line for part of his childhood. He went to a rural public school that had 18 kids in his senior class. His area of the country was very "behind the times" and didn't have nearly the resources that other schools had. Still, Justin chose to further his education more than most kids ever do: he worked hard at his grades, read *National Geographic* instead of playing video games, and joined academic and quiz bowl teams. With that, he was able to not only graduate at the top of his class with a 4.0 GPA, he was also able to score a nearly perfect 34 on his ACT. Most students with such limited academic resources would never become competitive on a national level. Justin worked hard and overcame his lack of resources to become one of the highest-scoring students in the nation.

See how it works? I took what Justin thought was a seemingly uneventful story, reframed it from a perspective he hadn't thought of, and painted a compelling picture that demonstrates admirable scholarship qualities like work ethic, drive, and achievement.

Everyone has a story. Take the time to really reflect on what yours is and what makes you unique. It doesn't have to be a tearjerker, and it doesn't have to read like anyone else's story to demonstrate admirable scholarship qualities. Judges can develop a personal connection with you even based on humorous stories and experiences. I just encourage you to take extra time, if needed, to really think of the best way you can effectively present yourself and "paint your picture."

Scholarship judges love to see what you're made of. They love to read about personal triumphs. **Though you may have things in your past that have brought you down for a period of time, what counts is showing that you will stand back up and fight to make things better.**

Always end personal essays with a positive or inspirational twist: explain how the situation has helped you grow or inspired you in some way. You'll show that you are deserving of the scholarship because you can handle trials gracefully, no matter what life throws at you.

Pulling It All Together

You've got your essay idea and direction. You've brainstormed and created an outline. Now it's time to piece it all together!

Keep these three essential tips in mind so you can connect the dots and create a winning essay: get organized, be consistent, and make an impact.

1. Get organized. Arrange your essay in an order that makes sense. That may seem like a no-brainer, but it's easy to get caught up in fitting everything you want to say into a small space while forgetting that the logical progression has to work. Make sure each essay has an introduction, a body, and a conclusion, even if each element is only a sentence or two. Imagine being a judge who doesn't know you and who is reading your essay for the first time. Is your writing clear? Does it flow? Think through how to structure your essays in the most reader-friendly way.

2. Be consistent. I have read scholarship submissions in which students say one thing in one part of the application and then completely contradict themselves in their essay. For example, without some kind of explanation it would seem contradictory if, in one part of your application, you talk about how your family struggled with poverty most of your life and then, in another part of the application, you describe how your world travels have broadened your perspective. Make sure when you look at *all* of your essay and application elements combined, they work together and are communicating a consistent, clear picture of who you are.

3. Make an impact. What is your essay's attention-grabbing potential? Have someone read your essay out loud to you and try to imagine it's your first time hearing it. Does it still pack the same punch you felt it did when you wrote it? Ask other people whose opinions you trust to read your essay as well and give their first impression. We're prone to get so focused on how hard we've worked on an essay that we forget to consider if it really has the potential to impact people the way we think it does. Seeking outside opinions is an easy solution. Also, constantly imagine yourself in the judges' position—with the number of essays they have to read—and then continually work to develop your content so that it will have a powerful, engaging effect no matter how many other applications get read.

REVISION AND REVIEW PROCESS

Few people write their very best work on the first try. Some of the most successful authors and songwriters will tell you the work that made them famous was their second, third, or even tenth draft.

Even if you feel like what you've written is pretty good, revisions can take it to a whole new level. The process of reviewing and revising your application and essays helps you find any grammatical errors, figure out better ways to word things, and get your points across more effectively.

Here's a proven method:

1. Read it again. After you've written your first draft of an essay, read back through it to see if there are ways you can improve it right now. If so, do it.

2. Walk away. Then, put it down for a few days. This will give your mind a chance to view it from a fresh perspective.

3. Read it again. After a few days' break, read back through your first draft and note what improvements you can make.

4. Walk away again. Repeat this process until you feel like you have a really solid essay.

5. Seek others' feedback. Once you feel confident about your essay, begin seeking outside perspectives.

One of the biggest keys to my success in seeking scholarships was asking people for help with the revision process. **Getting multiple perspectives encourages you to develop essays that really reach out and touch a variety of personalities,** *which is important because you don't know the judges.* Recruit your parents, English teachers, mentors, youth pastors, and others you respect to help you revise your work. Have them review your essays for structure, grammar, and the overall impact of your words. You might even give them your scholarship outline for the program you're applying to or the list of "scholar qualities" you are trying to portray (from chapter 6), and ask them to make sure you've hit each of those marks.

Start with asking just one person to review your essays. Once they've given their feedback, review everything and decide on what, if any, suggested changes you want to make. Take your newly revised essays to the next person, and repeat the same process until you've received only positive feedback from a few different "reviewers." If you continually revise your essays until they move everyone who reads them, there's a good chance they will also appeal to the scholarship judges.

Asking for Help

There is no embarrassment in asking people you trust for help in the revision process. In fact, it is still one of the most important techniques I use today. In writing this book, I relied on my trusted sources to help me identify areas for improvement as well as places where I needed to expand or reorganize the material.

View these people as keys to your scholarship success. Because they are!

PACKAGING

Have you ever been in an argument with someone and completely flubbed your words, only to later think of all the great comebacks you could have said? I have! In moments like that, I always wish I could go back and "repackage" my words.

While you're putting your scholarship application together, you have plenty of time to "package" and "repackage" your responses so you come across just the way you want. By *packaging*, I mean you take what you would like to write about and then present it using words that are *specific*, *appealing*, and *easy to understand*.

Most scholarship essays have strict word limits, so be sure to carefully phrase and package every word to make it count.

Think of packaging as gift wrap. It's always nice to get a present on Christmas, but when the gift is wrapped nicely with a bow on it—and it's intended just for you—it's more exciting than if someone just tossed some generic, unwrapped gift at you and said, "Here."

When filling out your application, you can create laundry lists of activities you've participated in and spout facts about your life and accomplishments, or you can "package" and "wrap" your words so that the scholarship judges are excited to read them.

Most scholarships leave ample room in their applications for students to list their activities, awards, and honors. Yet I also know it can be a bit intimidating to see all that space on the page, realizing you have to somehow fill it. In each category of the application, I recommend you start by listing the most important or appealing items first, and then work your way down.

If you are struggling to fill the space, there are strategic ways to package words that can make your lists seem a bit longer. For instance, let's say there's a blank for community service. Here's the Before and After language from an application:

Please share any community service activities you have been involved with in the past four years.

Before Packaging	After Packaging
Habitat for Humanity, Humane Society, Relay for Life, and Missions Trips	Helped build 8 houses with Habitat for Humanity. Walked dogs 2 times per week for the Humane Society. Raised over $700 to fight cancer by walking for 24 hours with Relay for Life. Attended missions trips to New Orleans & Guatemala.

If you have a good list of items to fill in the blanks on your scholarship application, then you don't necessarily need to expand them. But if you are really struggling to fill space, putting a small explanation of the activities you're listing can help. This also works if you feel a small description is needed to get your intensity of involvement across. **If you're involved in more activities than there is space for, it is better to give a great description of the activities most important to you rather than trying to cram all the activities in with no packaging.**

Here are some additional Before and After examples that demonstrate the impact of packaging:

Before	After
Cross Country	Captain of Cross Country Team
Gymnastics Coach	Head Coach of Gymnastics Team
Missions Trip	Coordinated Missions Trip to Haiti

Examples of exceptional participation like these may go unnoticed if not spelled out a little.

Now let's look at some lengthier packaging examples that pertain to essays in particular.

Before Packaging	After Packaging
I've done really well in swimming. I have a good coach and am team captain.	The sport I have excelled in most is swimming. I've been blessed with a wonderful coach who has taught me the value of hard work and continually pushes me to improve. The growth and progress I've experienced have allowed me to become team captain. I hope to use this position to motivate and inspire my teammates to be the best they can be.
When I was 10, my mom died. I didn't know what to do. I've tried to be good because I know she'd want me to be. I still hope to make her proud, and going to college would have made her happy.	I faced several obstacles growing up. I lost my mother in a car accident when I was 10. Her death came as a shock to me. Since she was my best friend, learning to navigate life without her was a challenge I wasn't prepared for. Yet with wonderful memories of her in mind, I learned to press forward and strive to be the woman I know she'd want me to be. I have no doubt that graduating with a college degree would make my mother very proud.

HUMBLE SHAMELESSNESS

As I mentioned in chapter 5, remember to "sell yourself" when writing your essays. It is perfectly fine to toot your own horn and be shameless when sharing your accomplishments in your scholarship application. You do, however, want to be humble too. The way to do that is by giving credit where it is due and showing appreciation for the life you have. You want to be likable and grounded without holding back key information and accomplishments that make it clear you should be the winner of a scholarship. It may help if you keep this in mind: **Most scholarship judges will never get the chance to meet you in person. Therefore, you can't be shy about letting them know who you are and why you're such a great scholarship applicant!**

Recycling: The Great Timesaver

There's a bonus to carefully working through this process on the front end: once you've completed a few scholarship applications, it gets easier! Not only do you achieve a flow and get the hang of how it all works, you can do a wonderful thing called recycling!

Recycling application elements is very similar to traditional recycling. Just as you might recycle plastic or metal by passing it through a series of processes that make it usable again, you can do the same for your essays, letters, and more.

Once you've completed one or two applications, you will have a blueprint you can adjust for future applications. You don't have to think through and hash out all your activities again—you've already done that! So from here on out, you can copy and paste the information into the next application and modify or improve it as needed.

A big advantage of recycling is that it allows you to keep

refining your application components. As you go along, you'll see bits and pieces that could be worded better for stronger impact. Using the set of templates you have created from previous application forms makes filling out future applications much less time-consuming. It also simplifies the college application process itself because college and scholarship applications have many similarities. After filling out scholarship applications, you will have well-developed information you can use for college applications.

Take the Time to Customize

When recycling essays, make sure that you still take the time to customize each one to the program you are applying for. While recycling is meant to save you time and effort, don't let it hinder your ability to produce meaningful and focused content.

Recycling is a joy of the scholarship process. You've worked hard to put your first few applications together. Now, put them to work for you!

SUMMARY POINTS

▶ Creating an accurate and moving *self-portrait* requires reflecting on who you are and what has made you, *you*. Each section of the application should be treated as important as the next, as they all make a significant contribution and impact on the overall masterpiece you create.

- Learn to maximize your essay effectiveness:
  - *Getting the ball rolling* can be the hardest part of writing an essay. You have so much or no idea what to say, and don't know where to start. Tricks like doing *brainstorm bubbles* and *free writing* can help you gather your thoughts and get the words flowing.

  - Tips like: *making each word count*, *showing versus telling*, and *keeping it personal* help scholars develop essays that distinguish themselves from the numerous scholarship essays that judges read every day.

  - Make sure your essays are *organized* and *consistent*. Remember that every judge will have his or her own personality and things that catch his or her attention. Review your essays to make sure they have the *impact* you thought they did when you originally wrote them, and ask others to review them and offer feedback.

- *Packaging* is like gift wrap for your words. It's when you choose your words wisely and in a way that appeals to anyone who reads them, including scholarship judges that come from a wide variety of backgrounds.

- *Recycling* scholarship application components means you reuse parts and pieces of your application on future applications. Recycling is a very effective tool that, when used properly, can help save you time and give you the ability to apply to several more scholarships than you could have without it!

ACTION STEPS

O Schedule a time to reflect on your life story and what makes up your self-portrait. Take at least 30 minutes to write down specific events, challenges, and people who have shaped who you are.

O Look at the Scholarship Application Worksheet in the Resources section of this book. Practice writing each of the essays following the guidelines given and using the tricks you've learned in this chapter. You will likely be able to "recycle" these essays in future applications.

PARTS AND PIECES

The Often-Overlooked Elements That
Make or Break Applications

This is a conversation I recently had with a high school student a week away from a major scholarship deadline:

SCHOLARSHIP COACH: Who do you plan on asking for a recommendation letter?

STUDENT: I haven't really thought about it. Probably one of my teachers. I don't know . . . Maybe you could write me a letter!

SCHOLARSHIP COACH: I don't really know you very well. Do you have any information for me to base my recommendation on? Perhaps a resume?

STUDENT: Um . . . no. Should I?

The answer to that question is YES! Although this student had many great credentials and elements to help her stand out in the scholarship process, she had failed to take seriously two often-overlooked areas of the scholarship process.

After further conversation, I realized she didn't know how much she could do to influence getting stellar *recommendation letters* for her scholarship application. Like many scholarship applicants, she assumed a recommendation letter was nothing more than an "important person" saying nice things about her.

She also didn't realize that a *resume* could be more than just a list of activities and achievements she would send in with the rest of the required paperwork.

In this chapter, I'll show you how to get the most out of these two elements of the scholarship application—recommendation letters and a resume. What other applicants may overlook, you can use to make your scholarship application memorable.

Smart Recommendation Letters

Recommendation letters are a vital part of the scholarship application process. These letters are provided by someone who knows you well and can positively recommend you to be a scholarship winner. I like to call these people "recommenders." They are basically legitimizing your efforts and serving as witnesses to the claims you've made in your scholarship application. **You can communicate how wonderful you are in your application, and the judges may well believe you, but scholarship committees like to have some proof and outside perspective—and recommendation letters provide it.**

Don't underestimate the power these letters can have. Think

about a criminal trial in a courtroom. If a defendant is trying to prove his innocence and a credible witness comes forward to verify the defendant's story, the jury is much more likely to believe him. Recommenders are witnesses who put their name and credibility on the line to support your case. They can come from a wide variety of backgrounds and areas of influence in your life. In fact, that's a plus! Most importantly, you want to find people who will testify to your greatness.

FINDING GREAT RECOMMENDERS

So how do you find these wonderful people who will write a positive recommendation letter for you? First and foremost, consider people who know you well.

There is a common misconception that finding the recommender with the most important title will set you up for success, even if the person doesn't know you. Don't be fooled. **Judges can see though generic recommendations in which the writer doesn't have a personal connection to you. The best recommenders are people who are part of your life and have watched you grow.** These individuals are more likely to provide the most compelling letters. They can cite specific points in your life when you have exhibited admirable qualities, and they can give firsthand testimony about your qualifications.

Some programs will require that you have a teacher or school official submit a recommendation, but when your reference sources aren't specified, you can recruit coaches, employers, mentors, family friends, youth pastors, or other credible adults you're close to. Nationally competitive scholarship programs usually require two to four recommendations.

Begin by brainstorming a list of individuals in your life who could potentially provide great recommendation letters. Create a list of at least 10 to 15 people to ask to write recommendations for you. It's good to have multiple recommenders so you can have options to choose from. Different people will be able to attest to different scholar qualities and experiences you've had.

For example, your sports coach may be able to share about your teamwork and perseverance while your pastor could share more about your volunteerism and character. Depending on the qualities valued most by the scholarship you're applying to, one recommender may be better suited than another.

If you are still early in your high school career and can't come up with a solid list of recommenders, now's the time to begin cultivating those relationships. Which adults in your life can you build a long-term relationship with (through graduation or beyond)?

How can you get to know those people better and allow them to get to know you? If it's a teacher, ask if you can help him or her with grading or some other task. If it's a coach, take the initiative to work hard during the off-season and keep in touch with him or her about your progress. By the time you reach your senior year and scholarship applications are due, you will have a solid list of recommenders.

COMMUNICATING WITH RECOMMENDERS

How you communicate with prospective recommenders can greatly impact the results. Be aware of the five most important considerations involved in asking someone to write a winning recommendation letter for you: timing, providing information, being specific about your goals, minimizing work for the recommender, and sending a thank you.

1. TIME YOUR REQUEST CAREFULLY

You want to wait for the right time and place to kindly ask someone to write a recommendation letter for you. Make your request at least four to six weeks before the recommendation letter is due.

This gives the recommender plenty of time to fit your request into his or her schedule and really write the best recommendation for you.

Also, time your request so it's at an appropriate moment. Talk to teachers after class or at a time when they aren't as busy. If it's a coach, wait until after practice. If it's someone you don't interact with on a daily basis, try to set up an appointment to make your request. You can also make your request through e-mail or by phone; however, I strongly recommend requesting it in person.

Be prepared with what you are going to say, including a brief explanation of the scholarship or scholarships you are applying for and what the program is looking for in its recipients. Also, tell this person why you look up to and respect him or her, and why that person's positive recommendation means so much to you! **Exercise your best manners and presentation skills in this interaction to encourage a strong recommendation letter. Even if you see your recommender as a friend, everyone enjoys feeling valued and respected.**

2. PROVIDE APPROPRIATE INFORMATION

Presenting your information to recommenders, no matter how close you are to them, is important. Every time a recommender agreed to write a letter for me, I handed him or her a folder containing three things: a cover letter, a resume, and a means of sending or saving the letter.

A Cover Letter. This letter should state your appreciation that the person has agreed to write you a letter. It should also include information about the scholarship you are applying for, the format and deadline for submitting the recommendation letter, and a brief description of what is being sought in an applicant.

A Resume. Your resume should contain all your contact information, extracurricular activities, honors and awards, volunteer work, and anything else you feel is important for a selection committee to know about you. Later in this chapter, I discuss resumes in more detail.

A Method for Sending or Saving the Letter. This portion of the folder can be adjusted based on the requirements of the program you're applying to. For scholarships that use an online form, provide your recommender with the correct website address and necessary information. If the scholarship requires recommenders to mail the recommendation letter, provide them with a prestamped and addressed envelope.

However, if the scholarship allows you to handle the recommendation letters, provide your recommenders with an e-mail address so they can send you a copy of the letter they write in addition to the signed hard copy. You could also provide a thumb drive or an alternate method for saving the letter. That way, if you need another copy in the future, you will have one you can print off for the recommender to sign.

Communicate Your Focus

Make sure you communicate in person and in your cover letter any specific topics or areas you are focusing on in your essays. I would often even share my essays with my recommenders to give them a deeper understanding of who I am and what I wanted people to know about me.

3. BE SPECIFIC ABOUT GOALS

It helps to share with your recommenders the ways they can help you in their letters. A lot of times, if you are close to a recommender, he or she may ask if there is anything specific you want included. Be prepared with an answer.

If they don't ask, make sure your cover letter paints a clear picture of what you are hoping to portray as an applicant. You don't want to dictate what the recommender should say, but mentioning some background about the scholarship program and what the program represents can help your recommender tailor the letter in that direction.

Also, be clear about the deadline and when you will come to pick up the requested material. And include the deadline in your cover letter as well. Don't put it on the recommender to remember.

4. MINIMIZE WORK

If you are applying to multiple scholarships, you will most likely use some of your recommenders more than once. Some scholarship programs have pre-drafted recommendation forms that must be filled out, while others require a signed letter. Each time you need a recommender's help, you want to make it as easy as possible for him or her. If the person has already written a letter for you and you would like to reuse it, reprint the letter so he or she just needs to sign it.

5. SEND A THANK YOU NOTE

Recommenders are writing letters as a favor to you. They don't get anything out of it other than the sheer satisfaction of helping you succeed.

Always follow up with a thank you note to the recommender. Not only will it make him or her feel appreciated for writing your letter, it will also leave the door open if you need additional or revised letters from that person.

Be sure to always express your appreciation to your recommenders in person too, not just in a thank you note! Take time to let each person know how much you value his or her leadership in your life and how thankful you are for the help.

The Scholarship Resume

A resume is a summary of your skills and experiences that are relevant to a particular application or job. Talk to anyone who's ever interviewed for a full-time job, and he or she has probably had to create and submit this document. But did you know that having all of your activities and accomplishments organized into resume format will benefit you greatly in the scholarship process too?

Once you've put in the time and effort to create a great resume, you can use it for many, many purposes. In fact, it's one of your best resources when filling out scholarship paperwork. A number of scholarships even require students to submit resumes highlighting their high school experiences.

Many templates and sample formats are available online for laying out your resume. Just make sure you set it up in a professional format.

Your resume should include relevant headings such as:
- Extracurricular Activities
- Work Experience
- Honors and Awards
- Leadership Experience
- Volunteer Experience
- Educational Achievements
- Enrichment Programs

Take plenty of time to reflect on the activities you've participated in that positively reflect your high school experience and your future goals. It's best if you start keeping an activity log early on in high school that tracks all the important events and activities you participate in and the honors and awards you receive.

You might even jot down some of the key things you learned in those experiences. You can then use that log as a reference to jog your memory when creating your resume; it will also help you fill in other parts of your scholarship application.

Despite the popularity of online resume-building sites and published books, don't get duped into believing your resume has to look like everyone else's. No two resumes are exactly alike. You need to follow the format that best represents you and highlights what you have achieved.

RESUME DOS AND DON'TS

Do . . .

- *Limit it to one to two pages.* Use a 10- to 12-point font that is easy to read. (Headings may be slightly larger.) One-inch margins are ideal.
- *Be honest and specific.* Only list things about yourself that are authentic and true. Seek to be descriptive and thorough but not too lengthy.
- *Be consistent.* Consistency in the way you format dates, punctuate, and use verb tenses creates an organized, professional appearance.
- *Use bullet points.* Bullets help the resume look concise and organized.
- *Keep it professional.* While there are various formats you can choose from, stick to a sharp-looking format

that is clean and organized. Extreme creativity is not valued in this particular part of the process.

Do not . . .

- *List personal information.* Avoid mentioning your age, marital status, religious affiliation, or sexual orientation.
- *Allow grammar or spelling errors to slip through.* Thoroughly review your resume for accuracy, and have others do the same. Spelling and grammar errors can suggest a lack of time and effort on your part.
- *Be too creative.* While I encourage creativity in most areas, your resume needs to be consistent with a scholarly presentation. Do not add photos of yourself or use odd colors or bizarre formatting.
- *Lie.* Don't expand or boost your resume with untruthful facts in an attempt to make it—or yourself—look better. Trust me, don't do it!

Once you have a solid resume, you can make it work for you. For example, you can pull the lists of extracurricular activities and achievements from your completed resume to use on your scholarship application. Just remember to tailor the information to the specific scholarship program you are applying for.

Your resume can also help when you're asking for recommendation letters or applying for colleges, jobs, or internships. A great resume is a wonderful tool you can use far into the future.

● ●

Visit TheCollegeNinja.com to check out a sample resume.

● ●

SUMMARY POINTS

▶ *Recommendation letters* help validate what you've shared in your application and give judges an additional perspective of you. You want to submit letters from individuals who have had a significant impact on your life and are willing to vouch for how wonderful you are.

▶ *Your scholarship resume* is a power-packed page on which you summarize and highlight your high school experience. It summarizes the activities, work experience, awards and honors, volunteer experiences, and educational achievements that have prepared you for college.

ACTION STEPS

○ Gather recommendation letters
   – Create your list of 10 to 15 potential recommenders.

   – Create "recommender folders," including your cover letter, resume, and a method for sending or saving the letter.

– Set up meetings with your recommenders to request your recommendation letter at a time that is convenient for them.

– Make your request!

O Brainstorm and write down all the elements that belong on your scholarship resume. Decide on the best format for your resume, and then begin inserting all of your resume elements following the tips discussed in the chapter.

9

FINDING YOUR VOICE

Succeeding in the Scholarship Interview

Few scholarship programs require students to go through a personal interview, but for the programs that do, it is usually a very important part of the selection process.

For example, when I became a Coca-Cola Scholar, there were two levels of scholarship winners: regional and national. The company flew all 250 finalists to its headquarters in Atlanta for an interview. The 200 regional scholars would receive $4,000 scholarships, and the 50 national scholars would receive $20,000 scholarships. The final decision was based on the finalists' interviews.

The original applicant pool included more than 100,000 students, and while being in the top 250 was an honor regardless of the final award, the difference between being a regional and national winner was $16,000! That's huge when you realize how long it would take a student to earn that much money working at a fast-food place on campus. And it all came down to a five-minute interview . . .

Secrets for Speaking Up and Standing Out

Have you ever wondered how some celebrities, CEOs, and politicians are so natural and engaging in interviews? Do you think they were all born with the ability to open up about their lives to millions of listeners or viewers? Probably not. Most of those people have spent hours practicing and preparing to be able to "naturally" answer interview questions. The good news is, so can you!

Preparation and practice are central to interview success. They're also what will help you be more at ease in those unpredictable moments. Preparing for pageants gave me countless hours of interview run-throughs before entering the scholarship process. I continued to work on my skills prior to leaving for my Coca-Cola Scholarship interview. Being able to go into that interview well practiced and confident in my abilities allowed me to walk away with the $20,000 prize! Strong interview skills also opened several doors for competitive internships and job offers in college. Developing your interview skills can reach far beyond the scholarship process, serving you well in the rest of your life.

INTERVIEW PREP

To get a leg up on the competition, apply these simple strategies to your own interview preparation: research the organization, review your application, focus on selling yourself, and bring along samples of your work.

Research the Organization. Just as with the application process, start your interview preparation by getting to know more about the organization you are hoping to impress.

- Does it place a high value on technological innovation, volunteerism, leadership, community development?
- What causes does it support?
- Have any significant current events affected this organization recently?

Knowing what an organization values can help you anticipate what the judges are looking for and the direction the interview may go. It also gives you the ability to answer what seems to be a broad or generic question in a way that highlights the qualities they value. Browsing an organization's website and brochures, as well as your own Internet research about the organization, is a fantastic way to equip yourself with this information.

Review Your Application. It's amazing how fast time passes when you're hustling to apply for scholarships. Before you know it, you're being flown to a scholarship interview and it's been three months since you looked at your scholarship paperwork.

Because the application is the primary tool the judges have to base your interview on, you want to make sure you know your application like the back of your hand:

- Go over every extracurricular activity, volunteer project, essay, and answer you submitted.
- Reflect on the experiences you cite in your application, remembering what made each one special to you, what kind of impact you had in the situation, and what you learned. This review will more easily enable you to recall experiences from your life to answer the judges' questions.

This may seem like a simple and obvious area in which to prepare, but students often fail to review their own material. They end up spending the interview trying to recall what they wrote instead of passionately speaking about the things they love.

Sell Yourself. Let me say upfront that being humble, gracious, and natural in your scholarship interview is essential. Now I'll follow that by saying: *sell yourself!*

When you're given the opportunity to sit in front of a panel of judges who are waiting to hear something memorable from you, don't be shy. Be open about your stories and experiences that make you special. **Judges WANT and EXPECT to hear about the wonderful things you have done to get to where you are! So don't hold back.**

As I advised you to do in chapter 5, think of yourself as a product and the judges as investors. What "features" do you have that are going to make them want to invest in *you*? This is your sales pitch—but now you get to present it in person!

If you are naturally shy or reserved, spend a little extra time preparing prior to the interview. Get comfortable with describing the experiences that have most influenced who you are. This will make it much easier to recount those stories during the interview and sell yourself in an authentic way.

Bring Sample Work. Don't forget to bring samples of your work for the judges to see, just in case. With scholarships that are based in the arts or technology, a strong sample piece can leave a lasting impression on the judges.

And maybe it goes without saying, but make sure your sample conveys excellence in a way that will leave a desirable impression. If it's not your best work, it could actually be more detrimental than helpful. Don't pressure them about leaving a sample, but if the judges ask, it's good to have something available.

PRACTICE, PRACTICE, PRACTICE

Practicing your interview can pay off big-time when you're facing scholarship judges. Make the most of your practice time by preparing in specific ways: anticipate your answers to standard interview questions and then conduct mock interviews with yourself and then with friends. Next, seek out leaders or public figures who might seem intimidating to you and ask them to help you simulate "game day" interviews. Finally, learn how to pay attention to details such as communication cues to convince the judges you have the knowledge, poise, and determination they're looking for in a scholarship winner.

Anticipate the "Regulars." Some questions consistently come up over and over again in interviews. I like to call them the "regulars." These are standard interview questions such as:

- What is your greatest strength (or weakness)?
- Where do you see yourself in 10 years?
- Why do you want this scholarship (or job)?
- How would you describe yourself?
- What is your greatest accomplishment?
- Tell us about an occasion when you overcame an obstacle.
- What is your family like?
- Tell us about a leadership experience you've had.

Since these questions are so common, it helps to anticipate how you would answer them in your interview. Prepare an outline with bullet points hinting at how you would want to answer each one. Only list a few words with each bullet point; judges want to hear authentic answers, so *do not* try to memorize your perfect answer. The bullet points will help you really discern and access the core of what you believe, but how you express it each time will vary.

Even if you are not asked an exact question on your "regulars" list, a lot of other questions stem from these core questions. The discipline of working through the regulars will give you ideas to grab onto when you are asked trickier questions.

Do Mock Interviews. With any sport or task, the more you practice, the better you become. The same principle applies to interviews. Answering random questions about yourself can feel awkward at first, but after several runs, it starts to become second nature.

Interviews require a different way of thinking than what you're used to in everyday life. They require you to think very quickly on a deep level. With practice, your brain gets better at doing it, allowing you to effortlessly respond to whatever is thrown your way.

Start by interviewing yourself. **Begin practicing your interview skills even if you don't have an interview scheduled yet. The sooner you begin practicing, the better you'll be when an important interview does come up.**

- Do an online search of "interview questions" and compile 20 more outside the "regulars" you've already made bullet points for.
- Print the questions, cut them out, and drop them into a bowl or basket.
- Pull out one at a time.
- Read the question and answer it out loud as you would do in an interview.

I recommend practicing in front of a mirror and/or recording yourself on video. We can often be our own best critic. Take note of ways you feel you can improve.

When you become comfortable practicing alone, recruit someone to help you. Give that person your scholarship application and a list of sample questions, and ask him or her to interview you.

The single biggest reason I developed strong interview skills was because of the time my mom spent doing practice interviews with me. I was able to work through the awkwardness I felt when I first tried answering formal questions. I learned to stop fidgeting and control my nervous ticks. Through those rehearsals, interviews started feeling more natural and fun.

Start with Those Closest to You

Have your mom, dad, aunt, brother, or best friend interview you. It's easier to start with people you feel comfortable with and trust. Practice as if they were your "game-day" judges and seek to improve both your verbal and nonverbal communication. Allow them to give you constructive feedback so you can learn as you go. Don't get frustrated if you jumble your words at first. Stick with it, and you'll soon see progress!

Simulate Game Day. Before every major interview I had in high school, I intentionally sought out people who intimidated me—like the mayor of my small hometown and other prominent business figures—and asked them to conduct a mock interview with me. I wanted to create the emotions I might feel on the day of the actual interview.

I felt incredibly nervous each time I went in for one of these simulated interviews, but because I got my nerves worked out during those practice rounds, I was much calmer on the day of the real interview.

If you make it to the final round of a scholarship competition, I encourage you to try this: Make a list of people you respect, have access to, and who also make you feel a little intimidated—people like your high school principal, sports coach, boss, or business leaders in your community. Ask if they'd be willing to give you 15 minutes of their time for a practice interview. Then set up a meeting and treat it like a real interview.

Think of it as a dress rehearsal, where you not only dress for the part but also follow all game-day etiquette. **Getting as close as you can to feeling what it will be like on the day of your official interview will help calm your nerves and relieve some of the pressure.**

Pay Attention to the Little Things. There's more to the interview than just the content of what you say. When someone only has five minutes to gather an impression of you, details matter. There are small areas of communication you can practice to help your "details" reflect positively to the judges. The Communication Cues chart shows cues to tune in to and work on before your interview.

COMMUNICATION CUES

VERBAL Spoken words including tone, vocal inflection, and meaning	NONVERBAL Body language used to reinforce your verbal communication
Don't Ramble Stay focused and on topic. Avoid dominating the conversation. Let the interviewer speak.	**Listening** Show interest in the interviewer's words. Indicate you are paying attention through good posture and occasional nods. Stay focused and watch for nonverbal cues.
Be Enthusiastic Use a positive tone and vocal inflections when appropriate, indicating to the interviewer your excitement about the potential award.	**Gestures** Firm handshake. Don't fidget. Keep your hands in check, avoiding excessive use of gestures.
Gratitude Thank the interviewer for his or her time and for the opportunity to interview.	**Facial Expression** Maintain eye contact. Use engaging facial expressions. Smile whenever appropriate.

Game-Day Readiness

The moment has arrived. You've watched yourself answer interview questions in the mirror countless times. You've practiced for your friends, family members, and others. You've learned all the communication tricks. You are prepared. Now . . . take a deep breath and be yourself! If you've made it to the interview phase in the scholarship process, then the committee has recognized something great in you. Now you just need to show them that what they've seen is true. Here are some last-minute tips for dressing wisely and keeping your focus on the big day.

DRESS WISELY

First impressions matter. While you are not being judged on what you wear, you don't want your outfit to hinder the impression you're creating or to send a wrong message to the judges. **Most scholarship judges won't pay much attention to what you're wearing in the interview if it's appropriate, but they *will* notice if it's not.**

Appropriate scholarship interview attire should be business professional, meaning clean, put together, and not casual.

- Guys: Choose a business suit or dress pants and a shirt, tie, and sports coat.
- Girls: Select a classy dress, business suit, or business skirt/pants and blouse. I recommend avoiding hand jewelry—rings or bracelets—so you're not tempted to play with it subconsciously.
- Don't: Wear jeans, chew gum, expose large tattoos, or wear large jewelry. **Basically, avoid anything that will distract interviewers and leave them negatively remembering your wardrobe instead of positively remembering you.**

The day of your interview is all about you, so set aside the time to focus and get into your "zone."

- Avoid stressors and distractions such as unnecessary phone calls, texts, or e-mails.
- Do a quick review of your application about an hour before your interview to refresh your memory.
- Plan on arriving early, and give yourself plenty of time to get to your interview. The rule of thumb is usually to arrive 15 minutes early, but I always like to allow 30 minutes in case I get lost, need to go to the bathroom, or run into any traffic jams. **Most interviews are at larger facilities with plenty of places to hide for a moment alone. Having that moment to take a deep breath and "get in the zone" before the interview always proved invaluable to me.**

Follow these suggestions and you'll be prepared for a stellar performance at your scholarship interview. Be passionate and heartfelt about the things you believe in. Show your authentic, natural personality, and let the real you shine!

For more interviewing tips and tricks, visit TheCollegeNinja.com.

SUMMARY POINTS

▶ Practice and preparation are the keys to a successful scholarship *interview*. Though an interview is not always required in scholarship applications, when one *is* required, it is an extremely important factor.

▶ *Simulating game day* by dressing the part, going to an unfamiliar location, and having a prominent person ask you questions can help prepare you for the stress of an actual interview.

ACTION STEPS

○ Go through the practice and preparation steps described in this chapter, even if you do not have an interview scheduled yet. More time practicing means better skills when an important interview comes up!

○ Set up a mock interview to simulate game day. Treat it like it's the real deal.

10

SWEAT THE DETAILS

Unleashing Your Inner Perfectionist

When your opportunity to share is very small, details are HUGE. In most scholarship applications, you only have a few pages to get your point across. Your content may be fantastic and your story engaging, but spelling errors, incorrect punctuation, and awkward wording can easily stand between you and a $50,000 award for college. Careless mistakes can send red flags to scholarship committees, signaling a lack of commitment to the process or just plain laziness.

While multiple edits and revisions may seem tedious, this area of quality control can be one of the easiest aspects of the application process to get right. Let's discuss how to make your application as bulletproof as possible.

The Power of Being Organized

The more organized you stay during the scholarship process, the less stressful it will be. With multiple deadlines and applications to keep track of, staying organized helps you feel more in control of the process. Practicing great organization skills now will also help you get things done quicker in the long run because you will be better equipped to multitask and complete applications efficiently.

Don't waste your precious time and peace of mind by scrambling for information and forms at the last minute. Stay ahead of the game!

Organization has not always been my strongest suit, but forcing myself to be organized in the scholarship process really paid off. I followed the three essential organizing tips every future scholarship winner needs to know: keep records, post deadlines, and start early.

1. KEEP RECORDS

Create a filing system to keep track of what you're doing. You can use a computer or good old-fashioned file folders. Start a new folder for every new scholarship you decide to apply to. Begin by putting your initial research into the file, followed by your breakdown of the scholarship's "ideal candidate," the application, recommendation letters, and any other relevant information. Having all your documents separated by application and in order will alleviate stress when you start to hit deadline crunches amid a busy schedule.

2. POST DEADLINES

Keep an active list of your deadlines posted somewhere that you'll see every day. Each time you decide to apply for another scholarship, revise your deadlines list, reprint it, and repost it. Also, keep your file system in the order of approaching deadlines. When you have mailed out an application to a scholarship program, move that folder to the back of the file system. You'll also want to set calendar alerts on your phone or computer for deadlines.

3. START EARLY

Try not to wait until the last minute to send in your application, because any unforeseen circumstances that arise—an illness or your computer crashing, for example—could derail all your hard work. The process is truly so much easier if you complete each step in advance and leave plenty of time. I did have my share of putting together a few last-minute applications, but the scholarships I found most important and that contributed the most money to my education took a little extra time.

Remember, being organized—keeping records, staying on top of deadlines, and starting early—gives you the freedom and flexibility to make mistakes in your first drafts and gradually arrive at your optimum essay and application. So why not make it easy on yourself? Excellence is within reach if you'll give yourself the time to make it happen.

Fine-Tuning

By this point in the application process, you've got all your thoughts on paper and you've worked hard to stand out, following the strategies for success described in this book. The most difficult part is complete, but now it's time to make sure the simple things are covered and corrected. Here are some critical areas to keep in mind as you do your final reviews of your application: spelling, grammar, and punctuation; missing and misunderstood answers; and word limits.

SPELLING, GRAMMAR, AND PUNCTUATION

Check and recheck for proper spelling, grammar, and punctuation. Not only is this practice important in your essays but also throughout the rest of your application. It would be unfortunate to have flawless essays and then not notice that your computer autocorrected your name to a crazy spelling. It's easy to miss incorrect spelling, grammar, and punctuation if you're not on the lookout for it. So make sure you, and at least one other person, check every area of the application.

MISSING AND MISUNDERSTOOD ANSWERS

Make sure you go through the application line by line to check that nothing is missing. It's tempting to say, "I'll come back to this later," but then forget. Leaving unintentional blanks could make you look inattentive or sloppy.

Also, read through each instruction and question more than once, making sure your response fits and that you haven't misunderstood what is being asked. It can be easy to think you originally answered appropriately, only to look back later and realize you misunderstood. After you've looked through your application yourself, ask your parent or another reviewer to look back through and double-check your work.

WORD LIMITS

Pay close attention to word limits. Though it can be tempting to squeeze just a few more words into your essays and think no one will notice, *don't do it*!

It's true that most scholarship judges won't sit there counting every single word to make sure you kept to their limit. Still, it could reflect poorly on your ability to follow directions if they do check. So don't risk it.

On the other hand, you want to take advantage of the space you have been given. If you have a 500-word limit, don't just write a 100-word essay. Being too far under the word limit could translate as a lack of effort or depth. Check each essay and make sure it fits appropriately within the word limits designated in the question.

Hone Your Essay

Honing means sharpening, and that's what you do when you delete unnecessary words. Your essay will be that much stronger if you'll continually cut words and "re-package" until it says just what you want it to say *within the word limit*. The honing process eliminates the mistake of being too wordy and helps create essays that pack a punch!

Mailing and Submitting

You've worked so hard to get to this point. You've completed your essays, your application looks professional, and you have stellar recommendation letters and a solid academic record. The last thing you want is for the submission process to jeopardize all you've accomplished.

When it's time to send off your application, double-check that all necessary application materials are included or have already been turned in. Make sure to follow up with recommenders or any outside source submitting a form for you, such as test scores, transcripts, or recommendation letters. Missing just one piece of information could disqualify you or put you at a significant disadvantage.

Here's what I suggest if you're mailing forms:

- Keep your paperwork clean and organized. Don't let it get wrinkled or dirty in any way.

- Be careful to organize your forms in the package in a way that makes sense. Place your application form at the front of the stack, followed by your essays, recommendation letters, transcript, and test scores.

- When mailing the most important scholarship forms, I always recommend paying a little extra money for delivery confirmation. There's great peace of mind in knowing the application you invested so much time in has arrived intact at its destination.

It also can be beneficial to call a scholarship program and confirm that all of your required forms have been received. I did this with most of the scholarships I applied to—and found out I was almost disqualified from my biggest scholarship because a fax I sent didn't go through.

The Importance of Review

Small errors stand out. There were several times when I thought my application was ready to go . . . and then I realized in my "final" review that I had left a space blank or a page was missing. With so few pages in the scholarship application and so little that the judges are basing their decisions on, you really want to make sure that you don't overlook anything.

It's okay to be a bit obsessive about your scholarship applications. After all, there are not only details involved in the process but also thousands of dollars on the line! Once you are confident that your application is as good as you can get it, submit it—and then *do not worry*. Celebrate its completion and move on to the next task. Until then, check and recheck your application and all of its parts.

SUMMARY POINTS

- A lot of details go into applying for multiple scholarships. Practicing good *organization* by keeping records, posting deadlines, and starting early can make the process seem significantly easier, less stressful, and ultimately save you precious time.

- Pay attention to the small, *easily overlooked details* such as spelling, grammar, and punctuation; missing and misunderstood answers; and word limits. Though they are very small, easily fixable details, they really matter when scholarship judges are trying to select one winner from thousands. Don't let silly mistakes derail all your hard work.

- When *mailing and submitting* forms, remember to keep them clean and organized.

ACTION STEPS

O Get organized! Create your own organizational file system. Having a plan and system set up before you are knee deep in scholarship applications will help alleviate a lot of stress and wasted time that comes with disorganization.

O Find someone, such as a parent, family member, or teacher, who will be willing to help you review your application(s) and check all the details. Sit down and make a game plan with him or her. Be clear about your vision and goals for the process, and clarify in advance what areas he or she can help you with.

CONCLUSION

No Holding Back

I'm not sure what your personal situation is, but just the fact that you've read this book tells me you are committed to earning a scholarship. That is the first and most important step. Becoming aware of how big an impact a scholarship can have and determining how hard you are willing to work for it are hurdles most students never get over. Whether it's because of fear, doubt, laziness, or naïveté, the brutal reality is that relatively few students ever give the scholarship process their best effort, and in turn, they miss out on life-altering opportunities.

What has held *you* back?

What has weighed you down in life?

Where do you want to be in 10 years?

Use your answers to motivate and drive you toward your success. These are the things that make you real, authentic, and capable of overcoming. It's not about being a perfect student or coming from a perfect family. You don't have to be a winner in everything you've tried. You do, however, have to be motivated, driven, and ready to succeed.

What I've Learned

As you've read, in the years before college I felt like life had really kicked me around and tried everything it could to make me feel like I wasn't good enough. I worked really hard and always tried to be positive, but I fell on my face over and over again and thought about giving up on several occasions. I was afraid my life would always be just one setback after another to get through.

Thanks to God and my family, I was never without the strength to stand back up. It wasn't easy, and it didn't always happen right away, but eventually I'd dust myself off, put on a smile, and try again. As lonely or frustrated as I sometimes felt, the dream of better days outweighed the hurt of the situation I was in.

To get through the dark moments, I'd listen to songs that made me feel better, vent my frustrations in my journal, pray for a new beginning, and remind myself of where my life could go. I'm so glad I hung on and worked hard through that season of my life. The Gates Foundation, Coca-Cola, my university, and other scholarship programs saw my potential and offered me a new beginning. I can look back at the struggles now and see how each one made me stronger and more capable of success in the future.

In it all, I learned that the scholarship process isn't always easy, but it can be fun and extremely rewarding. I'm not going to lie, though: receiving my first rejection letter stunk. I know from firsthand experience that when rejection happens, it's easy to let insecurities creep in and start doubting your efforts.

But don't be disheartened! It happens to the best and most successful scholarship applicants. Just keep going, keep your head up, and don't let rejection discourage you or scare you. Fearlessly learn from your mistakes and always ask yourself, *What can I improve?* Use the lessons you learn to continually fine-tune your applications and increase your chances for future success.

Yes, it can feel risky to put a lot of time and effort into the scholarship application process, but the rewards last a lifetime. You can't put a price on the value of a great college education and the experiences you gain from it.

The emotional roller coaster of waiting for responses can be nerve-wracking, but let me tell you how *great* it feels when you do get that letter in the mail that says, *You win!* In that moment, all the hard work and perseverance make sense, and it's clear what the journey was for.

At this point in life, the only person who can stop you is you. No one else can take away your drive, motivation, or ability to succeed. Starting today, use the setbacks you've experienced so far to propel yourself forward.

Happily Ever After

Why work so hard to go to college and get scholarships? What's the point? Is it worth the work? Well, statistically speaking, the average college graduate earns nearly $22,000 per year more than individuals holding only a high school diploma. On top of that, attending college without the burden of financial stress is truly a tremendous opportunity to grow and develop as a person.

After overcoming so many obstacles while growing up, it was wonderful to finally get a chance to breathe and enjoy my beautiful surroundings in college. Instead of trying to juggle full-time work in the midst of taking courses, making friends in my new town, and working toward a career, I got to truly focus on my education and building a new future for myself. While I didn't start off college with stellar grades, having my education paid for gave me the time to really figure out my academics. I was able to continuously improve my grades each semester until I eventually earned a perfect 4.0 in my master's degree program.

Outside of school, I also got to explore and pursue dreams, such as my love for music. While I majored in education- and business-related majors, I got to have fun traveling every weekend as the lead singer of a band. I got to network in the Nashville music industry, which allowed me to work with Hall of Fame and Grammy-winning producers, musicians, and songwriters. I also got to start a small marketing company, working for a variety of Fortune 500 companies.

Not only did college provide me with a wealth of opportunities for career progress, it also allowed me to grow tremendously as a person. I got more involved in church, developed a stronger personal relationship with God, and found healing from the wounds of my past. I made incredible friends who are friends for life. I also met my Prince Charming, who completely swept me off my feet! Now, I truly get to live out my "happily ever after" as I continue to pursue my dream career and start working toward my doctoral degree.

I tell you this so you can see the freedom and benefits that can be gained from working hard to attain scholarships. It can be life changing! My desire is to help you achieve even greater success than I have. First lady Michelle Obama described my feelings perfectly when she said, "When you've walked through that doorway of opportunity, you do not slam it shut behind you. You reach back and you give folks the same opportunities that you had to get ahead." I pray this book can give you what you need to launch yourself into the wonderful life you are destined to live in your future!

You Can Do It Too!

So many things can get you down and make you feel like you can't succeed. Too many families across the country have faced devastating financial losses and are now struggling to pay their day-to-day expenses, let alone the extra cost of college. People's lives have been ripped apart by natural disasters, home foreclosures, job losses, and the death of loved ones. Some of you wake up every day dreading school because you're bullied into feeling worthless. Some of you live in homes that feel like war zones, where there is constant fighting among those you love most.

But there is a light at the end of your tunnel—the light of a brighter future. No matter how dark or desperate your situation is now, stay focused on that light and keep moving forward. Or even if you can't see the light now, believe that it exists and faithfully run toward it, confident that you *will* reach it.

Now is the time to take all the challenges, heartbreaks, and struggles you've been through and use them to launch yourself into positive change. When you finally attain your dreams and accomplish your goals, you'll be able to look back at the journey and see how each challenge made you stronger, wiser, and more capable of getting to your destination. No matter what situation you're in now, you are capable of affecting your future. I hope this book has armed you with the tools and strategies to help you get ahead and set yourself up for success.

Stand up and seize the opportunity. Start writing down your goals and working through your action steps.

Continually visualize where you want your life to go and begin working hard to get there.

I have no doubt you can achieve your dreams. And before you know it, you'll be sharing your story and helping lift other people out of their darkness and into a brighter future.

Just remember . . . *The choices you make now will impact you for the rest of your life.* I encourage you to *choose* the very best. Believe in yourself and your potential. You deserve success in scholarships and in life!

RESOURCES

Extra Stuff You'll Need

Scholarship Application Worksheet

This sample scholarship application is designed to help you start brainstorming and give you an idea of the information requested on typical scholarship applications. Answering these questions and filling in the blanks will help you identify your strengths and weaknesses. Go to TheCollegeNinja.com to print out more copies.

Preparing for Standardized Tests

Learn how to prepare for standardized exams from Jay Rosner, college admissions test expert and executive director of the Princeton Review Foundation. From what to study to how to study, Jay tells students the most effective ways to find success in the exam room.

Scholar Stories

Sometimes we just need to know that we're not alone and the only one struggling. This section reveals stories from successful scholars that overcame significant obstacles prior to college.

How Parents Can Help

Parents can be huge assets in the scholarship process. From organization, to research, to simply being the biggest cheerleader, there are many ways parents can help their students. This section reveals key areas in which parents and students can work together for scholarship success.

Scholarship Application Worksheet

Visit **TheCollegeNinja.com** to print out a copy.

Legal Name:_____

                Last Name   *First Name*   *M.I.*

Address _____Phone_____

City _____State ___Zip _____E-mail_____

Date of Birth _____

Current Cumulative GPA _____*on a scale of* _____

SAT and/or ACT scores _____

What college do you plan to attend next year? _____

Intended Major_____

Please list any sports, clubs, programs, and activities you have participated in during the past four years.

ACTIVITY   ROLES AND RESPONSIBILITIES

1._____   _____

                 _____

2._____   _____

                 _____

3._____   _____

                 _____

4._____   _____

                 _____

5._____   _____

                 _____

6._____   _____

                 _____

7._____   _____

                 _____

8._____   _____

                 _____

Please list volunteer work or community service performed within the past four years. Include total hours volunteered with each organization, not just the number of hours worked each week.

Kind of Work	Name of Organization	Dates of Participation	Total Hours

Please list any awards or honors you have received in the past four years. State the nature of the award and the year you won it (for example: Most Valuable Player, 2011).

1. _____   9. _____
2. _____   10. _____
3. _____   11. _____
4. _____   12. _____
5. _____   13. _____
6. _____   14. _____
7. _____   15. _____
8. _____   16. _____

Please list any jobs or internships you have held during the past four years. You have space to list up to five employers.

Job Description/Role	Employer	Dates of Employment	Hours Per Week

Essay

Please answer the following questions in 500 words or less. Give the answers considerable thought, as they will weigh heavily on the judges' decisions.

Discuss your short- and long-term goals. Are any of them related? Which goals are most important to you?

Discuss an obstacle you've overcome. How did you get through it, and what did you learn from it?

Please answer the following questions in 250 words or less.

Describe a specific activity or experience that has been important in helping you clarify your ambitions and goals for the future.

Describe a leadership experience when you made a significant difference in your school or community.

Describe how your family background has influenced your outlook on the world.

Briefly describe a situation when you felt you were treated poorly. How did you handle it, and what did you learn from it?

Is there anything else you would like to share to help us distinguish you from other applicants?

PREPARING FOR STANDARDIZED TESTS

Q&A with an Expert

I've explained in this book that you can amass large amounts of college scholarship money without outstanding test scores. However, this does not mean you should take standardized tests lightly. I did, and as a result, I had to work much harder to make myself stand out to college admissions and scholarship committees.

Although I *thought* I was taking these tests seriously at the time, I had no idea what steps were necessary to prepare for them and increase my scores. The secret is to realize that standardized tests for college such as the SAT and ACT aren't your average high school exams. They are long (three-plus hours), challenging, multiple-choice tests, and they can potentially result in thousands more dollars in money for college as well as admission into top universities.

After consulting with Jay Rosner, admissions test expert and executive director of the Princeton Review Foundation, which offers fantastic preparation resources for the SAT and ACT, I'd like to share some insights into preparing for standardized testing.

Q: How can preparing for the SAT or ACT help me?

A: Preparing allows you to:

- become more proactive and strategic in the test room;
- learn to pace yourself during the timed test;
- see short- and long-term improvements in reading, vocabulary, and math; and
- be more confident and calm during your tests because you've completed a good preparation plan.

Q: What's the first thing I need to do to start studying?

A: Start your study plan by taking a full, timed practice test. This will help you gauge where you are at the moment, revealing your strengths and weaknesses. It will also guide you in developing a strategy that fits your preparation needs.

Q: What are the best ways to study for these tests?

A: When you study for the SAT or ACT, you should try to replicate as much as possible the official test-taking environment, which is a strange room (sometimes a classroom, sometimes a cafeteria or other site) that is quiet but not silent (people cough, the proctor walks around, etc.). If you can study in a library, that's ideal. Your kitchen table may offer additional distractions, so you might want to seek a quieter place. No texting, no phones, no television, no food while you're studying because those things aren't allowed in the official test room. You can take a break (and you should) every hour when you study; try to study the SAT or ACT for no more than two hours at a time so that all your study time is effective.

Q: How long do you really need to prepare?
A: To answer that, imagine a sport that someone might participate in for a season while in high school. Usually the season lasts a few months, with practices running a couple of hours each day. Testing preparation can bring 100 times the benefit to you as sports—simply because so few high school students end up being elite-level athletes. So why not give your test preparation half the time and effort? If you'll devote 90 minutes of high-quality practice per day for five to six days per week for five to six weeks, you will almost certainly reap better results. Also, I recommend taking at least three or four practice tests.

Q: There's no way I can devote that much time to studying with everything else that goes on during the school year! What other options do I have?
A: Planning in advance helps. Although not everyone reading this has the luxury of devoting the amount of time I'm recommending *right now*, the beautiful thing about advanced preparation is that by planning ahead, you can strategically fit test preparation around your other scheduling demands. That means you can

devote your time to studying for the SAT or ACT during your summers and your least busy times of year.

Make a study plan that works for you. If you find it impossible to devote 90 minutes to studying each day, push yourself to do what you can. Surely everyone can carve out at least 30 minutes a day to study for a test that can have such a big impact on his or her life. Improving your scores isn't a mystery; it just takes a little work.

Honestly, this is one of the most important tests of your young adult life. So treat it that way. While I've shared in this book that great test scores are not a necessity for you to win scholarship money, they definitely help—and even open several doors. Take the time to invest in yourself with a good study plan. It can really make a big scholarship impact!

SCHOLAR STORIES

The Winding Road to Success

Most of you reading this book have obstacles standing between you and your ability to go to college. Whether:

- your family doesn't support your goals,
- you don't feel smart enough,
- you weren't given opportunities that other kids have, or
- your family doesn't have enough money . . .

everyone faces personal challenges that can hinder his or her college dreams. That's why it's good for you to know you are not alone.

Confronted with these challenges, it doesn't take much to start feeling sorry for yourself; then you're vulnerable to making excuses and settling for less than you're capable of. The following personal stories from top national scholars demonstrate that success can be found in spite of significant obstacles. My hope is that by sharing stories of top national scholarship winners who came up against hard situations and fought to find success, you'll be inspired to conquer whatever obstacles are standing in your way!

Samson Lim

Gates Millennium Scholar
Horatio Alger Scholar

Weaving my way through a horde of defenders, I dribbled towards the hoop. Heart racing, adrenaline rushing, and legs churning, I heaved the ball into the air and crashed towards the ground. I landed awkwardly on my right ankle, twisting it badly. At that moment, basketball was the last thing on my mind. A tentative step confirmed my worries; I had sprained my ankle. It only took a few seconds, but those few seconds ultimately launched me into a spiral, a spiral that would spin my world upside down for the next ten years.

The next six months passed smoothly, or so it seemed, until I began having difficulty controlling my ankle. A trip to the doctor caused a domino effect of referrals to specialists. In fourth grade, I was diagnosed with dystonia, a neurological movement disorder caused by a genetic mutation and triggered by the sprained ankle. My childhood dreams of playing basketball evaporated. As time passed, my discomfort level increased. My ability to sit, to stand, and to walk—privileges I had taken for granted just a year earlier—became increasingly limited.

As muscle spasticity restricted my ability to partake in activities, my frustration began to build. Because of my walking troubles, I was forced to use crutches, and finally, a wheelchair in sixth grade. As a little kid, I had always wanted to sit in a wheelchair and have someone push me around. This time, I could not have wanted anything less. After my semi-confinement in the wheelchair, I remember how frustrated, angry, and upset I felt; however, my family, my friends, and my personality did not allow me to remain mired in a pool of depression.

Working hard at physical therapy, I began a slow recovery. Soon I regained enough mobility and strength to walk at school in seventh and eighth grade; however, upon entering high school, I had to rely on the wheelchair again because of the long distances between classes. During my freshman year, I had surgery to implant a metal pump filled with muscle relaxant into my abdomen.

The period immediately following my operation brought on weakness and an overall regression that discouraged me. I questioned my decision to have the surgery, but the continued encouragement of my parents taught me to have patience with my body's response to the new device. Sure enough, I improved within a few weeks, and my discomfort level dropped significantly.

Over the next three years, my condition continued to experience ups and downs. The summer before senior year, a new and improved procedure became a very real possibility—brain surgery. Initially, my parents shied away from the option because of the potential risks involved; however, the lessons I had learned from my previous experience instilled in me the strength and willpower to undergo the surgery. We flew down to San Francisco after the end of the school year, and I was admitted to the

UCSF Medical Center. Confronted with a nine-hour surgery including three hours of consciousness, I nevertheless felt confident in my doctor's ability to perform the operation. His steady hands implanted two electrodes into my brain and connected them with a wire to an electrical pulse generator implanted in my chest. The success of the operation is evident by my significant improvement. Despite my numerous scars and plethora of doctors' orders, the peace I gained gave me hope for the future.

After months of physical therapy, I am now fully independent of the wheelchair. My steady progress since my brain surgery has given me cause for optimism and hopefulness. Over the past decade, the trials and tribulations I have experienced have shaped my personality and molded my character. If I had never sprained my ankle in third grade and developed dystonia, I would never have learned to empathize with others, to have patience in difficult circumstances, to embrace the gifts others take for granted, and to remain optimistic despite the troubles of life.

THE JOURNEY TO COLLEGE

In spite of the challenges my body faced in high school, I was still determined to be involved in my school and go to college. My sophomore year I ran for vice president of a club as a joke, and surprisingly, I won. I seized the opportunity wholeheartedly and discovered that I really had a passion for being in leadership positions. I started a Model UN club at my school and joined the

Math Club, Knowledge Bowl, and National Honor Society. For senior year, I ended up being president of MUN again and also of Math Club, and I signed up as a Senior Class Officer.

I remember my parents always worrying about how they'd send me to college, especially with all my medical bills. During the summer between my junior and senior year, I determined to apply for as many scholarships as possible—and that I wouldn't stop till I had college all paid for. I was extremely lucky to have met my goal after about 75 applications in the spring of my senior year. I ended up with 18 scholarships total and turned down a few others too, since I had a full-ride already. I estimate that I spent between 400-500 hours applying to scholarships in four years of high school. Senior year, I'd come home from school and start searching the web for scholarship opportunities. It became kind of a game and an obsession. Winning scholarships, for me, meant I would be able to help my family by not burdening my parents with loans. It meant I was afforded the opportunity to truly engage in my studies, my university community, and to really make an impact. I didn't have to worry about working to pay my tuition, and I didn't have to worry about how I was going to have to pay off loans. It freed me from all this, so I could pour my heart and energy into making my community better.

For scholars struggling through difficult situations, I say, "Always have faith." It's always easiest to just give up, but the tough road can be the most rewarding. For me, I don't believe

God gives us any more than we can handle, and those who have been given much (i.e., put through the toughest hardships) have been given them because they can handle it. Looking back at my own struggles, I wouldn't trade them for anything, even knowing how difficult those years of physical anguish and discomfort were. They have made me who I am, and I am a better person for it. So, for scholars who are still struggling to see the light at the end of the tunnel, they should know—it's there.

July Lee

Coca-Cola Scholar
Discover Tributes Award Scholar

Emigrating from China without a high school education, my parents settled in Mexicali, Mexico and brought me into this world. I grew up with the Hispanic culture, assimilating into a world that clearly contrasted with the color of my yellow skin. Who I am today and how I got here are a result of my immediate environment and my family's way of upbringing. Although money was never overflowing in our home, there always seemed to be enough to get us by. Reality was, I grew up in a low-income neighborhood in Mexico where the roads were unpaved and the cockroaches were plentiful, but that came to no surprise as the neighborhood's dumpster stood in front of our humble abode. In the back of my mind, there is still the faint sound of the chickens clucking and the stray dogs howling into the desert night. Raised at a time before the Mexican drug war, the kids in our neighborhood roamed around freely and I quickly assimilated into a culture very unlike my own.

My father worked as the head cook of a Chinese restaurant in Mexico where his cooking skills were highly esteemed and his leadership valued. He always returned home to fill the house with mixed aromas from cooking at work all day. My mother, on the other hand, was a stay-at-home mom. In my world, she could do it all. The many years she spent plowing the rice fields of China and working in the clothing factories taught her the skills to sew our clothes and to harvest our food. In our backyard, she raised chickens and planted an admirable vegetable garden. After all, it was a cheaper alternative to spending money at the grocery store.

In 1996, we received our green card and immigrated to the U.S. when I was six. I felt like I was at the top of the world the moment I stepped in to see the white walls of our new tiny condominium. We moved into an immigrant town in Southern California along the Mexican-American border where nearly 97 percent of the population identified themselves as being Hispanic or Latino. While the traditional Chinese values were practiced at home, a step outside our front door presented a unique world into the Mexican culture. Embracing America as a true melting pot, this hybrid of experiences taught me many languages and cultural values. For my parents, immigrating to the U.S. was a wish come true, but we soon realized that experiencing the full grandeur of the glorified American dream would not be so easy. Living in the U.S. while still working under Mexican wages had its consequences. My father began working longer hours to make financial ends meet and crossed the border to Mexico every morning to get to work. We started living in our new home using blankets as mattresses, dirt as toys, and the view through the windows as a television set. However, our parents set the example, teaching us to pursue a hardworking mindset and to embrace our provisions. It was not until I suffered a loss that I began to realize the value of all the things I took for granted—my father's death.

One August morning, I woke up to the ringing of the phone as my mother took the call: "Ma'am, your husband is in the hospital. Please come as soon as possible." It was on the news—my father was a victim of an attempted murder during a robbery at a restaurant he worked for in Mexico. In the two weeks that followed, my father was placed on life support and suffered traumatic brain injuries. He was transported from Mexico to an immigrant border town in the U.S., but even there, the hospital lacked the doctors and the resources to adequately treat the severity of my father's wounds. On the day he was to be lifted by air to another major hospital in the U.S, I was allowed to see him for the first time. Feeling paralyzed as I stood by the bedside of an unrecognizable man, I could only muster the strength to let my fingers touch his fragile hands. That night he passed away, never waking up from his coma to see his wife and children for the last time.

Forced to take on the dual role of a parent after my father's death, my mother worked 70-hour weeks at minimum wages in Mexico as she struggled to sustain the living finances for four in America. So, at the age of 12, I joined the Mexican workforce, busing restaurant tables, selling shoes, and working at fast food places; on the weekdays, I crossed back to the U.S. to go to school. But it was in these environments where I began to grow and mature as a person. All around me were other street children working amidst trash and filth exposed to diseases. The likelihood of them receiving treatment and vaccinations were close to none. Men on crutches and injured teenage boys knocked from car to car and cleaned windshields, hoping to collect enough money to treat their wounds and make a living. Compared to them, I had so much more. What became clear to me then was that I needed to become someone who could selflessly make something out of that situation. Going to college to pursue medicine would be for me the practice of self-empowerment from which I could treat the disempowered.

Given my circumstances and the status of my community, I was expected to fail, but, determined, I developed a strong will to overcome the barriers. Perseverance and hard work paved the road ahead as I graduated as the valedictorian of my high school class and entered Stanford University, where the opportunities to further explore medicine at the local and international level exploded. My life experiences and my upbringing from three disparate cultures taught me the Spanish, the Cantonese, and the English that proved to be indispensable in my interactions with the people I encountered. Whether it was conducting health research in the rural villages of Nicaragua or lab research at the Stanford Medical School, the growing field of science never ceased to amaze me. When volunteering with the orphans of Mexico or serving in the typhoon-stricken region of Taiwan, I found fulfillment and joy.

Having recently graduated from college, I can look back and say that the obstacles in my life made me a much stronger person. In order to pursue my dreams, education was key. Given the financial circumstances of my family, I was driven and determined to apply for scholarships because I knew that money should never put a fence around my dreams. Learning from my experiences in applying to scholarships and writing essays, this is what I have to say: Do not be afraid to reflect on your life and become transparent about it on paper. Your story is uniquely your own and that is what makes it special. If there is one piece of advice I would leave with you, it would be the following: Never say you can't until you try. You are in control of your future and no one else but yourself can dictate the direction of your life.

● ● ● ● ● ● ● ● ● ● ● ● ● ● ● ● ● ● ● ●

For more scholar stories, visit TheCollegeNinja.com.

● ● ● ● ● ● ● ● ● ● ● ● ● ● ● ● ● ● ● ●

HOW PARENTS CAN HELP

Parents, as you may remember, the junior and senior years of high school can be *very* busy for active students! Finding little ways to take some of the pressure off can greatly increase the number of scholarships your son or daughter will be able to apply to, giving him or her more time to focus on filling out quality applications. In this way, you can become an excellent supporting character in the scholarship process, providing encouragement, motivation, and backup. Yet it is important to always empower your son or daughter to spearhead the process.

In the next few pages, I will describe some great ways you can help your student through the scholarship application process. Let your son or daughter complete the tasks I mention throughout the book, but understand that by supporting your student in the ways I suggest, you can do a lot to free up time for him or her to apply for more scholarships.

Search and Organize

Identifying the most fitting scholarships for your student is a great way you can help. With literally thousands of scholarship programs offering money to students each year, narrowing down the possibilities to the most suitable scholarships can take many hours of work. Search through the numerous resources discussed in chapter 4 for finding scholarships, and filter out the ones that aren't a great fit for your student. This allows your son or daughter to focus on applying for the more appropriate scholarships and increasing his or her chances for success.

Once you and your student have a list of scholarships to apply for, you can dig a little deeper to find out more about the scholarship programs themselves. Visit the programs' websites and search for information on previous scholarship winners and other helpful facts.

Helping your son or daughter stay organized is another way you can be very effective. Refer to the tips and tricks suggested in this book and make a plan with your student for how you can assist him or her.

Listen and Encourage

Applying for scholarships can at times be an overwhelming, emotional process. It requires a lot of thought—and sometimes results in rejection. Most people who have won a lot of scholarships have also lost several as well. Having someone there to listen, encourage, and bounce ideas off of through the process can be invaluable. Be prepared to allow your student to vent about the process, offer to brainstorm with him or her, and remind your student that the benefits of the process will be worth all the hard work.

Without my mom, I would not have gained the level of

scholarship success I did, and the journey would not have been as positive as it was. Your support—emotional and otherwise—can lead to a winning application for your student. Enjoy the process! It can be a real bonding experience for you and your teen!

Reviews and Revisions

The first drafts of applications and essays are usually far from perfect. While it is ultimately a student's responsibility to revise his or her applications and make sure the words flow well, you can help by reviewing the overall message that is communicated and checking your son or daughter's responses for punctuation and grammatical errors.

After filling out several applications, students can easily miss small errors. Give the application a fresh look and help your student catch anything he or she may have missed.

Interviews

Though not as common in the scholarship process, interviews are sometimes used to judge scholarship applicants. When a scholarship program does require an interview, it usually carries a lot of weight in the judging process. In chapter 9, I discuss winning interview techniques. One of the principles discussed is doing mock interviews. Parents can serve as great "interviewers," helping students build and develop great interview skills.

Push Through the Awkwardness

From personal experience, I can tell you that practicing interview questions with a parent can feel incredibly awkward and embarrassing at first. I eventually pushed through my discomfort, which allowed my mom to become a huge asset in my preparation.

When practicing interviews with your son or daughter, be patient and noncritical. The biggest purpose of these mock interviews is to help your teenager become comfortable in an interview setting. Give your son or daughter a safe place to learn, grow, make mistakes, and ultimately build self-confidence.

No-Crossing Zone

When helping your student in the scholarship process, it is important to never cross the "questionable" line. For example, if you're reviewing essays and applications, never cross the line of actually writing the essay or shaping it according to your perspective.

Here's a good rule of thumb: If you're ever helping your student and you think to yourself, *Am I going too far? Would it be acceptable if the judges knew I was doing this particular thing?* then you most likely need to take a step back. If there's any chance that what you're doing is questionable and may be frowned upon, *don't do it!*

Being supportive of your budding scholar is a great thing, but always encourage him or her to "be the star" and take the lead in the process. Look for ways to empower your son or daughter and make the scholarship adventure fun. As you and your student move through the process, continually be on the lookout for new ways you can provide effective support. Each parent-teen relationship is different, so I encourage you to figure out what works for both of you.

With desire and a little strategy, you can be the greatest factor in your son or daughter's scholarship success. I've written this book to help you and your student attain it . . . together.

Visit TheCollegeNinja.com

Find Helpful Tools, Information, and Inspiration

Scholarship Listings

Sample Scholarship Application Forms

Tips & Tricks

Scholar Stories

Instructional Videos

And more!

Win a One-on-One Mentoring Session!

Register at TheCollegeNinja.com for a chance to win a personal video-chat mentoring session with Kristina! Let her help you lay out your scholarship success plan and develop a strategy that works for you!

Facebook.com/TheCollegeNinja

Also, like us on Facebook
for frequent updates.

For more information on the author, visit:
KristinaEllis.com

• • • • • • • • • • • • • • • • • •

To contact Kristina for speaking
opportunities, media requests, or
interviews, please send an e-mail to:
Info@KristinaEllis.com

ACKNOWLEDGMENTS

God—Words can't express how much I love you and how thankful I am that you've been here for me all along, even in those times when I ran from you and didn't trust you. Thank you for loving me more than humanly possible and for being with me every step of my life.

Mom—If it hasn't been clear enough throughout the book, I'll tell you again: I love you and think you're the best mom ever! Thank you for giving up your life for me—for letting me grow up in the United States when you would have been happier in Venezuela, for working from home so you could be there for me, for sitting through hours of boring practices, and for always smiling when I looked up to see you in the stands. You were so selfless and dedicated in raising us, and I will always remember the sacrifices you made to make me who I am today!

Dad—Even though our time together was cut short, you made the most of the time we had and left me with so many formative memories to cherish for the rest of my life. Thank you for pushing through your pain during your battle with cancer, to make such a strong, positive impression on me. I wish you were here to see me today. I know you'd be so proud of your little girl. I'll never forget you, and I'll always carry a part of me with you. I love you, Dad, forever.

Mark—We've come so far together. You've always had my back and been such a motivator for me. You've helped shape me into who I am and have inspired me to go after big dreams. I couldn't be more proud of you and everything you are doing! Thank you for being my cheerleader, example, and friend.

Tonna—You've loved me like your own child my whole life, and I can't thank you enough. From coming to visit me every spare moment you had, to allowing me to ask you awkward questions about boys and life, to literally saving my life in one phone call, you've dropped everything to be there for me more times than I can count. You've always been such a role model, encouragement, and friend to me, and I know I wouldn't be here today without you. Thank you.

Duane—Even though I hadn't known you very long when my dad passed, you stepped in and were there for me more than anyone could ever expect an uncle-in-law to be. I'll never forget being nine and you talking to me about economics, politics, and business. Even though I had no clue what you were talking about at the time, in so many ways you were shaping my thinking, and

I'll forever be deeply grateful for that. Thank you for being such a positive male influence in my life.

Slate—Thank you for being my best friend. Not only have you encouraged, supported, and motivated me at every step of the writing process, you've sat with me for hours—brainstorming, editing, and proofreading every single page. You have gone so far above and beyond to support me in this dream, and I don't know if I'll ever be able to express how truly grateful I am for you. You are such a blessing in my life and to this book!

Grandma and Grandpa Ellis—To the only people who have officially seen every single place I've lived since I was in college, thank you! I am so grateful for all the times you made the four-hour drive to visit and remind me how much I am loved. Your 50+ trips to Haiti set a shining example of what it means to serve the world and give back. Your constant love and support of me are constant reminders of my dad's heart. Thank you for everything you've done throughout my life to help me get to this place.

David Sams—You saw the vision for this book and believed in me from our very first conversation. The book would not have been possible without you, and I'm so thankful for everything you've done to make it happen. Thank you for all the times you helped me brainstorm, sold others on the purpose of this book, and shared your incredible advice. You've been a mentor, business partner, and friend at every step, and I'm so thankful for everything you've done.

Kris Bearss—You are the best executive editor anyone could ever dream of! You definitely went above and beyond. Thank you for pushing me to dig deeper within myself and share my story with students, and for always being there to answer my questions. I didn't know that writing this book would lead to such a beautiful friendship, but I'm so thankful for it!

Chance—I don't know if you realize how much you helped me write this book. You have been a constant reminder of my purpose and passion for creating this book and helping students. Thank you for trusting me and allowing me to walk through life with you. I know God has huge plans for you and that you are going to have a powerful impact on the world. I am publicly declaring that I will ALWAYS be here for you, and I feel so blessed to get to help you through in any way I can!

Worthy Team—I feel so fortunate to have each and every member of your talented, supportive team backing this book! You captured the vision for this project from the beginning and provided me with everything I needed to bring it to fruition. And you didn't just work to put out another book; you truly became passionate with me about reaching students and making this difference. Thank you for believing in me, for believing in the book, and for surrounding me with help at every stage of the publishing process. I truly feel so blessed!

Book Contributors—I want to say a huge thank you to everyone who contributed knowledge, research, stories, and information to this book. The body of information I was able to compile would not have been possible without the students who filled out surveys, the scholarship administrators who allowed me to interview them, and the scholars who shared their stories with me. Thank you so much for supporting me in this process and for sharing your wisdom and experience.

IF YOU ENJOYED THIS BOOK, WILL YOU CONSIDER SHARING THE MESSAGE WITH OTHERS?

Mention the book in a blog post or through Facebook, Twitter, Pinterest, or upload a picture through Instagram.

Recommend this book to those in your small group, book club, workplace, and classes.

Head over to facebook.com/mykristinaellis, "LIKE" the page, and post a comment as to what you enjoyed the most.

Tweet "I recommend reading #ConfessionsofaScholarshipWinner by @mykristinaellis /@worthypub /#scholarshipconfessions"

Pick up a copy for someone you know who would be challenged and encouraged by this message.

Write a book review online.

You can subscribe to Kristina's e-mail list at
KristinaEllis.com

WORTHY®
PUBLISHING

Visit us at worthypublishing.com

twitter.com/worthypub

facebook.com/worthypublishing

instagram.com/worthypub

worthypub.tumblr.com

pinterest.com/worthypub

youtube.com/worthypublishing